BEAST FACTORY

BY
KERMIT CANNON

2011 recipient of the President's Council on Fitness, Sports & Nutrition Community Leadership Award

ILLUSTRATIONS BY BRIAN GARCIA, A.K.A. "TAZROC"

PRAISE FOR BEAST FACTORY

"Great Book!"
    – Keyshawn Johnson
    Super Bowl Champion, 3X Pro-bowler

"The *Beast Factory* is more than a tool to get you into the best shape of your life, it is a mindset. A mindset where you embrace training as part of who you are. This book changed the way I approach training because it taught me the value of putting quality, not quantity time in the weight room. I don't think I get to where I am today without the routines that transformed me from a high school kid who didn't understand what it takes in the weight room to succeed, into someone who now welcomes and enjoys a training opportunity."
    – Geoff Schwartz
    Carolina Panthers Offensive Lineman

"The concepts from this book really helped me take my abs to another level."
    – Morris Chestnut
    Actor

"A very beneficial and innovative approach to student athletes success."
    – Lovell Houston
    National Director of the Student's Council on Community Health

"Whether you're trying to get in shape or take your fitness to a new level, Kermit Cannon is the perfect guide to helping you discover your inner beast."
    – Patricia Manuel
    USA National boxing champion

"I lived through the *BEAST FACTORY*! During the summer before I attended Oregon University, I trained with Kermit using the beautifully illustrated routines in this book hoping to be a walk-on football player. These training guidelines gave me the edge I needed to ultimately earn a scholarship! There is a method to his madness!"
    – Max Forer
    Oregon Ducks
    2-Time Pac 10 Champion Center

"This is a very needed tool in the proper and healthy development of youth athletes."
    – Daniel Graham
    #86 Tennessee Titans
    2X Super Bowl Champion

"The Beast Factory is a Extremely well-written phenomenal book! It breaks down your fitness in a useful, clear, informative way, and you get great tips. This book covers ground in a readable, comprehensive, fun way! I highly recommend The Beast Factory for your fitness and nutrition."
    – Christine Spence
    Team USA 400 meter hurdles

"What a way to make a difference in your life, with this easy and well designed 12 week program. With a little hard work and dedication you will be well on your way to getting in better shape."
    – James Cooper
    New York Yankees
    Minor League Outfielder

Beast Factory: A twelve week illustrated guide to transforming yourself into a toned, more powerful, quicker animal!

Publisher/Author note:

Illustrations and cover design by Brian "Tazroc" Garcia are © 2011 (www.tazroc.com). Illustrations may not be reproduced without permission

Book design by Dana Jones, LookBookPlus.com.

Visit www.youth-sports-training.com for more resources.

Welcome to "Beast Factory." There is a beast in each and every one of us. The beast is that animal inside that pushes us to keep going when we are hurt, tired or simply lazy. Maybe you have decided that the time has come to unleash your beast. Whether you are trying to get in shape or take your fitness to a new level, this book can be your guide to help you do that. If you make a commitment to use the blueprints in this book to transform yourself you will see results that can change your lifestyle and your life.

I have been designing workouts for youth, teens and adults since 1993 and have been fortunate enough to train athletes that have gone on to gain college scholarships, play professional sports and serve in the military. This book is a 12-week blueprint to building a better you. All 48 routines should serve as goals to be completed in one hour or less. The weights suggested are just benchmarks. You should adjust the numbers to challenge yourself to help you achieve your own fitness level. Always concentrate on perfecting your form to decrease the possibility of injury.

Want to eat healthier and feel better? The diet and health tips in this book are very powerful tools that are easy to understand and use. The routines are designed to optimize your body's ability to burn fat and build muscle. The remarkable airbrush illustrations and the descriptions of the exercises make it easy to understand even for beginners.

Congratulations on your investment to improve your life by entering "The Factory". Now is the time to unleash your beast!

DEDICATION

This book is dedicated to the hundreds of students at Santa Monica High School that had the heart, desire, and determination to complete the "Beast Factory" workouts with me on campus over the years and the coaches, parents and teachers that believed in me.

My 3 amigos: Rob Duron for his friendship, guidance and advice; Tebb Kusserow for his friendship, wisdom and integrity; and Norm Lacy for his friendship, leadership and inspiration (You will always be missed)

ACKNOWLEDGEMENTS

Writing **Beast Factory** has been a long, incredible journey. Much appreciation to Brian "Tazroc" Garcia, one of the most talented artists in California, for the illustrations. Thank you for being my partner in this project. Much thanks to Shawana Isaac and her company E-Architext (www.e-architext.com) for her countless times of assistance including: webpage work, editing, artistic insight and attention to detail. This project would have been almost impossible without you. Lee Schwartz for his guidance, feedback and advice. Thank you for helping me with the 'business side' of this project! Geoff, for inspiring me to train youth full-time. Max Forer for never giving up. Gina Wong, for your flier work with the SPARQ project and constant encouragement.

Michael and Melissa Harney, who have helped me see the "bigger picture". Dylan Harney, a true hero who inspires me to never quit. Susan Salter Reynolds, your help, direction and advice was invaluable and gave me the inspiration to dream bigger. Thank you to all the parents and teachers who were brave and trusting enough to let their children participate in the voluntary Beast Factory Boot camps. A special thanks to my sister Kelli for her unbelievable artistic talent and input in all of the Youth Sports Training projects. Her Husband Hymon for his excellent video work. My parents, who didn't even know I was completing this project but support me in anything I do anyhow.... Deidre for always being supportive and helpful. Nikki, for her faith, character, love, support and loyalty.

BEAST FACTORY
CONTENTS

STARTING THE ENGINE

Around two-thirds of America is overweight. Although we realize that exercising keeps us healthier, makes us look better, and relieves us from some of the everyday stressors, we still make up excuses not to do it. Imagine if your parents walked you out to the garage and gave you the keys to a new car and said: "Take great care of this car because it is the only car you will ever have in your life!" You would probably use the best gas and fluids available, change the oil regularly, get constant maintenance and repairs, and keep the interior nice. That is how our bodies are. We get one to work with. There are only so many synthetic pieces, valves, silicone and collagen people can add to their bodies before the whole machine breaks down.

Muscles allow us to make tackles and baskets, score goals, swim, and look really nice at the beach. While most people tend to notice those biceps and abs, it's the hidden muscles deep inside your hips, shoulders, and core that make them stand out. Working these areas benefits your entire body and gives you more strength, helping you avoid injuries. While lean muscle mass allows you to function every day and helps to give your body a great appearance and shape, muscles are also your broiler, cooking up fat. Your muscles act like garbage disposals. They need to grind the body for calories in order to keep themselves full and growing so they end up churning and burning the calories we eat. By adding a little more muscle to your body you will burn calories throughout the day. Each pound of muscle you have uses up to 50 calories a day just to keep it going, so if you add 6 pounds of muscle you will burn up to an extra 300 calories a day. At that rate you can burn off 30 pounds of fat in a year!!

This book focuses on working the 2 major muscle groups: the big muscle groups and small muscle groups. The big muscle groups include your legs, chest, back, and shoulders because that is where you can build the most muscle in the least amount of time. When you work larger muscles you increase metabolism and burn calories longer. The small muscle groups, and cardio, give you that chiseled look by working your "quick-twitch" muscles, combining balance with lifting. Most of us want to be strong and lean, but still toned and muscular.

FINE TUNING

Your body reacts to cardiovascular exercise the same way it does to music. If you hear a slow, love song, you might be tempted to call that ex that you have been avoiding. If you hear something that is high in energy with a great bass line or guitar riff, you can't help but 'pump it up'! While there is a time and place for the slow stuff, the gym or track is not it. Your body reacts better, in terms of fat loss, when you engage in cardiovascular exercise that is high-energy and intense.

This book is not about spending as much time in the gym as you spend on your cell phone. It is about spending enough time to build lean muscle mass and change your shape enough to build some muscle that will burn fat by itself. Your body's motor oil is glycogen. It uses this stored glucose as the main source of energy. You won't use this energy by sitting around all day, but as soon as you start a major workout your energy level is on the clock. Start by keeping your weight lifting workouts an hour or less. After a certain amount of time in the gym your body starts producing a hormone that blocks testosterone and wastes muscle. Once your energy and performance starts to break down you have already received most of the benefits of the muscle group you have been working, so all of your extra work might be wasting your time.

Try to rest for 60 seconds between sets but don't be too concerned about specific rest periods between sets. Instead rest as you need it, more as your muscles become tired, and less in your early sets when your muscles are fresh. This way you will cut your total workout time by 15 to 20 percent.

You have to analyze your workouts that you are doing and also see your problem areas. You have to look at yourself and say, "I have to improve on this specific thing". You can never be totally content with yourself. Once you take control of your time, you will have the strength to attack your biggest challenges. Failure is just a small detour to success. It shows you how far you have come and how far you need to go. This book does not produce formulas, but rules to live by. If you know why something works you're more likely to do it right and often.

Make personal records for yourself and log them in a notebook. Try to lift more total weight each week, it's the key to building muscle, improving strength and increasing endurance. The longer you've been lifting weights, the heavier the weights need to be in order for you to see results depending on your age.

If you don't like an exercise, you should start doing more of it. You are probably not doing it because you are weak at it. Test yourself often. Every 4 weeks measure your waist size, chest size, body fat, or something that shows your journey to the goal. This will let you know the results of your training, and that translates into motivation.

SHIFTING GEARS

Muscles get bigger and stronger when they are introduced to new exercises and techniques. If you look around your gym you will see people who are still doing the same exercises they learned in their first workout program. Their muscles will not grow to their full potential. Exercises can expire just like milk, bread and bad breast implants. Changing your training approach is the key for opening the door of a frustrating fitness ceiling in either muscle growth or strength. If you have been lifting consistently for a year or more, you should change the look of your workout which can enhance the look of your body. A weight-training program that never changes can create strength imbalances which can be unhealthy and unproductive. By changing your workouts, your muscles will constantly have to adapt. As a result your performance will never peak. By simply altering your grip or your stance in a lift can stimulate new growth.

Sometimes machines can build muscle better—for instance, when you need to isolate specific muscles after an injury or when you're too inexperienced to perform a free-weight exercise. Certain free-weight exercises copy athletic moves and activate more muscle mass. If you are an experienced lifter, free weights are your best tools to build strength and burn fat. Sometimes you need to overhaul your routine to get your body to the next level, just like we overhaul our wardrobe to get out of the last decade...

TRAIN SMARTER, USE DUMBBELLS

Don't let the name fool you. The reason that most of the weight exercises in The Beast Factory involve dumbbells is because there is no piece of equipment that is better at building muscle, versatility, and effectiveness than a pair of dumbbells.

In many gyms you see dumbbells only being used for curls. In this book they are used for every muscle group in you body including: legs, back, arms, shoulders, chest, and core.

The versatility and different angles and grips you can use allow dumbbells to challenge your muscles more than a barbell. There might be 20 or more variations of a shoulder raise you can do with dumbbells, as opposed to much less using a bar and even fewer on a shoulder machine. Dumbbells keep challenging your muscles and keep them growing because of all of the different routines you can do with them. When it comes to range of motion and getting bringing more muscle fibers to the party, barbell can limit you by coming into contact with part of your body during a lift. When you hold dumbbells in your hand, you can bring them lower in a repetition. You will train smarter using dumbbells because they help you find out where you have imbalances in your strength. For example, if one arm is weaker than the other or was injured in any way dumbbells will not let you cheat by over-compensating with the other arm to lift the weight like a bar or machine will. Each arm must work independently, working those all-important muscle stabilizers to prevent injury and keep your body in balance.

EQUIPMENT FAILURE

Don't exercise when you are sick unless your illness is all in your head. Even if that is the case, you still might be better taking a day off. Before you skip that workout, determine how sore you really are. If your muscle is sore to the touch or the soreness limits your range of motion, you should give the muscle at least another day of rest. If you're not sore to the touch and you have your full range of motion, go to the gym. You should have an "active rest" day which can involve light aerobic activity and stretching, and even light lifting, which can help eliminate some of the soreness. This light activity stimulates blood flow through the muscles, which removes waste products to help in the repair process. Start with 10 minutes of dynamic warm-up and then exercise the sore muscle by performing no more than three sets of 10 to 15 repetitions using a light weight. Your body will use its energy to heal itself and not build muscle and endurance. When you are recovering from a muscle injury you should begin exercising again as soon as possible. Try doing smaller sets making it easy to test yourself. Go slowly with no explosive movements. If you feel any pain stop immediately. After your workout ice the injured area for 20 minutes and exercise again the next day. You should be able to go a little harder and longer each day.

If you don't get enough deep sleep your muscles cannot recover. When you work out and don't get your "Zs" you exercise at a lower intensity than you think although your mind thinks it is higher so your muscles are less likely to receive enough stress to grow. Go to bed and wake up at set times every day even on weekends to keep your sleep cycles regular. Avoid caffeine which can throw your sleep patterns off.

HOW MUCH WEIGHT SHOULD I USE?

The sets in this book are simply a guideline. Focus on total reps for each exercise and compare the sets you do to the guideline. If it takes you twice as many sets to complete the repetitions you are using too much weight. Although the routines have suggested weights to use it is fairly simple to find out how much weight you should use. Pick the heaviest weight that still allows you to complete all of the repetitions in the sets. If you are doing all the repetitions in 3 sets instead of the suggested set of 5 you need to add more weight. You have to find these amounts by guessing and experimenting. By the third set of a new exercise you should know the proper weight. Be sure and write it down for the future. It should be easy to realize when the weight you are using is too heavy. The reward for finding the right weight is a better workout because you are doing more work with your biggest, strongest muscle fibers.

Count your repetitions backward. When you are near the end of a set your mind will tell you how many you have left instead of how many you have done. Increase the weight by the smallest amount possible every week. This will guarantee progress. Every person on every lift has a sticking point: that part of the repetition at which they are the weakest. If you find yours and strengthen it you will be able to lift heavier weights which will make your muscles work harder and grow faster. This point is easy to locate: It is the point at which your movement starts to slow down and your form breaks down. You have to count on the "Beast" in you to gauge if it is too light by pushing yourself to a level of discomfort. Go hard or go home…

Depending on your goals you may want to train in a slower, more controlled fashion. Other times when you want to generate as much power as possible, move as fast as you can. When you are trying to develop power, you will want to lift in an explosive way. When you are trying to develop strength and stability, you will want to move in a slower, more controlled manner. Both styles are very efficient and effective. Most people believe that you are supposed to lift weights slowly and under control. Lifting weights under control is a must in order to keep your form perfect, but the faster you lift, the better the results.

If you're trying to increase muscle size, fast lifts activate more of the muscle fibers that have the best chance to grow. If you're trying to become leaner, fast lifts do more to speed up your heart rate and lengthen your metabolism than anything else. You must also increase your cardio training to at least two to four times a week to help burn away excess body fat in order to become leaner. Alternating the way you do cardio keeps the workouts fresh. Try and mix in running, rowing, cycling, swimming and other exercises. Try and keep the cardio days and strength workouts separate so you will not sacrifice strength and size. If you are doing them on the same day, choose a lift that focuses on a different body part than the cardio portion of your workout. The best increases in strength are achieved by doing the 'up' part of the repetition as quickly as possible. Lower the weight slowly and under control. You have a greater chance for growth during the lowering phase and when you lower with control there is less chance of injury. If you're trying to grow stronger watch a Strongest Man Competition or Olympic lifters. None of their feats of strength are performed slowly. The lifts might take a long time to develop because of the amount of weight but the athlete performing the feat is trying like hell to get it done as fast as possible. A fast lift with a heavy weight uses more muscle fibers than a slower lift with a lighter weight but those big, strong muscle fibers tire quickly—usually in 15 seconds or less.

Your body has two ways of telling you when these muscle fibers are exhausted:
1. The speed of your repetitions slows.
2. Your form breaks down and you either shorten the range of motion the exercise requires or cheat to accomplish the full range. When this happens you should end the set rather than keep going with slower speed or bad form. Some strength and power exercises include medicine balls that will allow you to speed up a load without worrying about slowing down. An example would be throwing a medicine ball against a wall as hard as possible as if you were swinging a bat or golf club. This is impossible to duplicate in a weight room with weights.

TOO MUCH DAMN WEIGHT!

Don't work your muscles to the point at which you can't do another repetition and your form breaks down. This isn't the best way to get bigger and stronger. Most people are thought to have an equal number of slow- and fast- twitch muscle fibers. Slow-twitch fibers are mainly used for endurance activities and fast-twitch fibers are engaged when an activity takes more maximum strength. Sprinters, football players and basketball players are blessed to have more fast-twitch fibers than others. Long distance runners, cross-country skiers and distance swimmers have more slow-twitch fibers. Fast-twitch fibers are larger than the slow ones and can get even bigger. Slow-twitch fibers have the potential to grow also. The closer you get to your strength limit the more fast-twitch fibers are involved. As your muscles begin to tire they use fewer fast-twitch fibers. These fibers are responsible for bigger size and greater strength. For most exercises you should use a weight that allows you to finish all of your repetitions. If you can't you are using too much damn weight!

It is a common mistake to try to lift more weight than you can handle. It's natural to try and be better than someone else. (If we can't have their looks, money, car, boyfriend or girlfriend, we can at least out lift them!) The only way lifting heavy weights can benefit you is if you lift them with good form. One thing to look for is that the barbell is parallel to the floor. If it is leaning to one side you're applying more force with one arm or leg than the other or your grip is not aligned properly and consistent throughout each repetition.

Your fear combined with ego can be another thing to block you from achieving your goals. For example when you squat you must lower your body until your thighs are parallel to the floor. If you are using too much damn weight you might not go down that low for fear of getting "stuck" so you "half-ass" it and return to the starting position.

If you can't complete your entire set without the help of a spotter, it is too much damn weight! You should have a spotter for safety on certain exercises not to help you get through a workout.

If you can't hold on to the bar without wrist straps you are using too much damn weight! Some people use straps on the bar to hide their weak grip strength. You are better off using weights you can hold without help. This will force your grip strength to improve along with muscle size and strength. If you start lifting without straps you will be lifting more than you ever could with them.

Check your clothes, hair or make-up out in the mirrors at your house, not in the gym. Mirrors are in gyms for a reason and these are not the reason. Mirrors are there for you to make sure your form is correct so you don't get injured. If you sway and swing back and forth like a drunk person when you do standing curls or your lower back arches like a St. Louis Monument on bench presses, arm curls, squats, dead lifts and rows, you are using too much damn weight!!

EXCUSES TO REMAIN OUT OF SHAPE AND SKIP WORKOUTS

• It makes me feel special to have my clothes custom made

• Only fatty foods taste good

• I'm waiting until the New Year to make a fitness resolution

• I can use extra flesh folds to hide things

• Fast food restaurants require no reservations or fancy clothes

• Oatmeal does not compare to Fruity Pebbles

• Fitness people are airbrushed

• Workout sweat is gross and funky

• Fitness instructors are egotistical bastards

• Round is a shape

• If exercise was good for you it would not hurt

• I don't have to worry about sharing the arm rest on airplanes or in movie theaters

• Why would anyone need to see their own "private parts" anyway?

• I eat for people in poor countries that can't

• Everything tastes better fried or with cheese

• My cannonballs in the pool are much more exciting than yours

• Walking to the donut shop is exercise

• The mirrors in the gym make me look fat

• I hate working out by myself

• I have too many chores to do

• I have too much homework

• The gym is too crowded

• Gym memberships cost too much

• 'American Idol' and 'Dancing with the Stars' is on TV

DON'T BE A FLAKE...

t is your choice to continue to be lazy, fat, skinny, or weak. But every workout routine you miss can cause you to get fatter, shrink your muscles, make them weaker and most importantly, shorten your life. Unfortunately most young people exercise their right not to exercise. These ideas can help you stick to your plan to get in shape:

• Sign up for a sporting event and pay for it in advance.

• Make a bet with someone you compete against, envy, or simply don't like.

• Work out with a friend who will stay on you about showing up for a workout but not one who allows you to back out of workout plans.

• Discover a sport or event that you enjoy and train to compete in it. This will make you train harder for the sport or event. Try something in your school or a local park league.

• Listen to your favorite adrenaline-boosting songs when you exercise. This will also cut down on "gym-chatting", a main killer of exercise-routine flow.

• At the start of the month put all of your workouts on paper or computer and cross them off as you finish them. If you don't finish any of them at the end of the month add them onto the next month

• On the lazy days when you don't even feel like getting off of the couch plan on doing just one set of your favorite exercise. Most likely once you have started you will finish.

• Buy a year's worth of Whey Protein and store it where you will see it everyday.

• When you get to the gym, do the exercise you despise first. This will not only motivate you to complete the workout, but will also make all of the ones following seem less-challenging.

MISTAKES TO AVOID

Entering the weight room is the first step toward building muscle but it's not the last. What you do before, during and after a workout can either destroy your hard work or elevate your growth to a new level. Your personal habits, your social life, even which exercises you choose to do can take away from what you're trying to build.

You know smoking is stupid. You know the risks of developing cancer, a stroke and other health issues even if it is just from those cool "TRUTH" commercials. You should also know you are killing your strength training if you smoke. Smoking places carbon monoxide in your system which prevents your muscles from getting as much oxygen to use for energy. The less oxygen your muscles have to work with the less efficient they will be at contracting which cuts down their ability to work.

If you smoke try to quit smoking. Try using doctor prescribed or over-the-counter methods of quitting as a last resort. Getting in at least 30 minutes of exercise three or four times a week not only helps control body weight but can also produce positive psychological effects that might take away your addiction to smoke.

Nippin' at the bottle can cover that 6-pack you were hoping for with a sloppy keg and interfere with hormones that help build them. Drinking alcohol on a regular basis can also lower your testosterone levels more than usual in men and decrease muscle mass.

ALL THE RAGE

In most gyms in America there are men and women working out as hard as they can to do the workouts they read in a bodybuilding magazine hoping their results resemble the super-hero figures of professional bodybuilders demonstrating the exercises. Their attempts to get these bodies without steroids better known as the "juice" is like trying to win the Kentucky Derby with a Chihuahua. Unfortunately even the people not using enhanced substances are trying to follow these routines which can be frustrating when they don't get the results they see in pictures.

One of my missions is to show you a way to train drug-free using a different approach to get the best results for your body type. You won't look like Conan the Barbarian but you will be in better shape than your were before and much healthier. So why do some lifters spend thousands and risk their health and freedom by traveling across the border to get many forms of steroids, including those meant for horses? Because natural testosterone is a key ingredient to building muscle. Like most men love to look women's breasts, steroids are the breast implant versions of natural testosterone.

This synthetic product:

• Speeds up the body's ability to convert protein into muscle

• Creates new muscle cells and causes these cells to expand giving them the ability to hold more protein

• Incinerates fat cells

• Allows users the ability to train longer and harder

• Allows the body to recover faster between workouts

Now the downward spiral side. The side effects of steroids can be both devastating and embarrassing:

• "Shrinkage". Unfortunately for men, the head with the brain can get unusually large but the testes surrounding the other head can get unusually small…

• Acne patches that Proactive can't even cure

• Baldness (this one is for the ladies…)

• Huge breasts (this one is not for the ladies…)

• Overgrown and unproportioned muscles

• Increased risk of liver disease, heart attacks, stroke and cancer

• The super-aggressive behavior that causes you to go from David Banner to the "Incredible Hulk" known as "'roid rage" (where you beat up your best friend…)

Today's society places our sports and movie heroes in a light that makes a lot of people desire to be stronger, bigger, quicker and better looking. Don't be sucked in to an endless desire. Once you start taking steroids and your body stops producing testosterone you will have to take even more to get results. This endless cycle leads to a disappointing end.

DON'T BE A GYM RAT

A day at the Beach

To work the little muscle stabilizers around major muscle groups, do plyometrics on soft surfaces. This strengthens those muscles and improves their reaction time. This will result in huge gains when you jump or run on a harder surface. Running and jumping on sand is low impact so it is easier on your joints, improves your balance and makes your core and legs work harder by adding instability. Sand also helps build ankle and foot strength and burns over 60 percent more calories than running on a harder surface.

Biking

I visited a gym at the beach and watched in horror as members rode stationary bikes looking at the view of the ocean!!! While stationary bikes perform some aerobic assistance you can just get off when you lose motivation. Ride a bike along the beach. If you get tired you have to ride back or stick your tail between your legs and call someone to throw your bike in the trunk of their car. Unlike your local spinning class, biking can give you a great back workout. Find a big hill to ride and stand up on your pedals the entire way. Biking is also a great low-impact aerobic exercise. You will get a lot of the same benefits as running. It also spreads impact between your arms, legs and butt, helping to preserve those knees.

Boxing and Martial Arts

Boxing training classes can improve your speed, resistance, reflexes, flexibility and strength without the black eyes and bruises. Boxing workouts help improve your balance and coordination. These physical benefits you gain from boxing and kickboxing are just few of the many benefits that

they can provide. These workouts are great ways to get rid of stress and anger. You don't need to hire a cut man but I suggest you get instruction from a boxing trainer to learn proper techniques so you don't injure yourself.

Hiking

Hiking is a great way to get out of the city and restore, heal, and invigorate you. Finding a long, beautiful, challenging trail can make your body stronger and your mind quicker. Most of us are isolated from our natural, healthy state. Trade in the hum of a treadmill for the symphony of humming birds and the snaps of twigs and leaves under your feet and get rid of some anxiety. Paddle boarding

Paddle Boarding

Stand up Paddle Boarding is a growing sport that offers you a fantastic overall workout. You must use both strength and balance to keep from falling off and propel yourself through the water. This cross-training sport will engage the muscles in your legs, arms, back, stomach and even your feet. Just like swimming and surfing you won't experience any pounding on your joints or muscles and it is also a non-contact sport unless you have some serious wipeouts....

Pilates

Pilates emphasizes movement starting from the center of the body and developing core strength in the deep muscles of the center to stabilize the trunk and protect your back. Adding Pilates sessions to your workouts not only strengthens your core but also increases the number of pushups you can perform.

Recreational Sports

There is no one overall rule to getting fit. Spending all your time in a pool, on a track, or in the weight room may not be for you. Recreational sports burn calories too. Join a local sports team, play golf (Don't ride in the fancy cart! Carry your clubs…), play tennis, go hiking, build something, or start a band. All of these activities can help you stay in shape along with a fitness program.

Row Your Boat (or machine)

Few sports or exercises develop both power and endurance. Rowing works the most muscles and burns the most calories than most aerobic exercises. Rowing also works the muscles in your back and can improve your posture. The strokes in rowing work all the major muscle groups: legs, core, and back. The muscle tissue that connects the bottom of your lats is essential in helping to stabilize your spine. This helps transfer power between the muscles in your lower and upper body when you row.

Running

Running about 20 minutes on the days after your weight-lifting sessions can help you recover from your workouts faster. Too much running can alter your body from gaining strength and muscle. Don't run or cycle the day before a weight workout in which you plan do a weight lifting leg routine. Running causes muscle fatigue and damage just like weights. Your scrawny legs need time to recover! Research has shown that higher-intensity workouts promote weight loss better than activities like running 3 or 4 miles at the same pace (which can get boring anyway…) You can do a light run the day after a leg workout to help speed your recovery and reduce the soreness but a hard run will probably undo everything you did in the workout. Don't train for a triathlon, marathon, or any other endurance event while you're trying to build serious muscle and strength. You can train for both endurance and strength throughout the year, but not at the same time. Have you ever seen a heavily muscled marathon winner??? There is a reason for that…

Swimming

Swimming is a great cardiovascular exercise with none of the impact, joint-pounding of running. Since water is 1,000 times denser than air, you can burn the same amount of calories in the same amount of time that you are on a bike without getting hit by a car. No need to get fancy with the strokes unless you think you are Michael Phelps…. The freestyle stroke will do. It provides a great cardiovascular workout and works more muscles overall than any other strokes. Swimming helps build the core muscles in your chest, back, and abs.

Surfing

You don't have to grow long hair and become a beach bum to get the benefits of surfing. Surfing has a reputation as a slacker sport but it is far from that. This sport allows you to get an aerobic and anaerobic workout in the water. What you don't see in a surfing contest is the time surfers spend paddling. Chasing waves is like arm aerobics and can help tone up and build your shoulders. You might not get as good as Laird Hamilton but you can master your balance and increase your overall athleticism.

Yoga

Don't think you need to be able to wrap yourself into a human pretzel, join a cult, or become "one with your belly button" in order to do yoga. Yoga is a ancient practice that links your body with your mind as well as help master your breathing. Joining a yoga class can speed up muscle recovery, increase overall strength and boost energy.

ENGINE PARTS

Abs can be a little like our distant cousins: We know where they are, but who really sees them or remember what they look like? That is because ab muscles can be covered in a layer of fat that is dangerous because of how close it is to our organs. Ab exercises alone do not remove this fat but we still cannot skip these exercises. By working your abdominal muscles you will build them so that when you do burn fat your abs will stand out more than a fresh zit in the middle of your forehead. More important than that, abdominal exercises help you build a center of strength that will not only turn a few heads but make you healthier and stronger in the long run. If you gain strength in your core, you gain it in your entire trunk area, not just the 8-pack of muscles in the front. There is a very strong connection between smaller waist sizes and better health. When you develop your abs and shed fat your entire body becomes healthier. This reduces the risk of heart disease, diabetes and other types of diseases. Abs protect you more than any other muscles in your body so a strong core affects how your entire body functions.

Arms

Like shoulders, arms get work when you work all of the other upper-body muscle groups. Many people put too much focus on making their guns pop out instead of focusing on the larger muscle groups and finishing up with a few bicep, tricep, and forearm exercises.

Back

You need to stretch the back muscles in to the maximum to develop a big back. Lifting without your back is like speaking without your tongue.

It can happen but we won't know what the hell you are saying.

Chest

Everyone likes a nice broad chest. It is a large muscle group that is almost eye-level and looks great in the mirror. Unfortunately the chest is one of the first muscle groups to shrink after you stop lifting weights. This happens because chest muscles are rarely used in daily activities. In sports this muscle group is important for pushing opponents, tennis strokes, baseball throws, and punching.

Core

Your core consists of the muscle groups that run up and down and around the torso from your rib cage to your hips. These muscles often work together to perform everyday tasks such as bending, lifting and twisting. You must develop a strong and stable core if you expect to become a strong squatter. Movements like standing shoulder presses and bent-over rows require serious core strength to stabilize during these exercises (especially when lifting heavy). If you play any sport that requires movement, the most important muscle group is not your biceps, chest, or legs. It is your core. Developing core strength gives you power. It strengthens the muscles around your entire midsection and trains them to provide the right amount of support when you need it. If you play start-and-stop sports like basketball or tennis, strong abs can improve your game by helping you get from point A to point B faster than your opponent. The stronger you are the faster you get to the ball or a point on the field or court. Stronger Abs can help you prevent back pain. In most cases back pain is caused by weak muscles in your abs. Maintaining a strong trunk can improve many back-related problems. The muscles in your core don't work alone. They weave throughout your torso like a spider web, even attaching to your spine. When your abdominal muscles are weak the muscles in your butt and along the back of your legs have to work harder. This core weakness causes instability in the spine and eventually leads to back strain and pain or even a more serious back injury. Squeeze your glute (butt) muscles when you lift weights over your head. This will force your body into a position that will automatically stabilize your spine, which can also help prevent back injuries

Legs

Developing the largest muscle groups in your lower body -- your quadriceps, hamstrings, and glute or 'butt' muscles -- will boost your metabolism by increasing your body's lean muscle mass. This development also increases the body's production of hormones that help you build muscle. If you don't train your legs your hamstrings will become weak causing your hips to tilt forward. This will place too much stress on your lower back.

Most people tend to skip working the quadricep muscles because the most beneficial exercises to develop them, the squats and lunges, are some of the most difficult of all. Squats are known to burn more calories than any other exercise and are exhausting. Don't cheat your legs by doing the leg-curl machine and think you are working all of your quad muscles.

Every time we walk, run, or stand we are activating are glutes and hamstrings. The problem is most of us spend too much time sitting so get up off of your ass!!

Shoulders

Great shoulders not only make your upper-body look toned and stronger, they are the easiest to define because it is one of the last places the body will look for to store fat. Shoulders will develop faster than other upper-body muscles because they are involved in chest, back, bicep, and tricep exercises.

DIET (FEEDING THE BEAST)

Our society is fat. We eat too much. We eat bad foods. We will fry all the good nutrients out of vegetables. This is why people in our countries have bellies the size of small hybrid cars. The problem is not just eating fatty foods but also being inactive. Fast food is not representative of its name. It will not make you run fast.

Sometimes your stomach is growling and all you want to do is reach for the closest object that will fit in your mouth. Just because you think you are hungry does not mean you really are. Eating the wrong thing at the wrong time can add pounds you've worked so hard to lose.

I have seen a lot of people that are trying to change their eating habits have one bad meal and continue to go south for the entire weekend or a few days. Don't let one meal define your diet. You should not assume that you have failed your program. Instead follow up a "cheat" meal with at least five healthy meals and snacks.

Clean out your house of junk food and then re-stock it with almonds and other nuts, cheese, fruit and vegetables, lean meats and fish. By eliminating snacks that don't match your diet and providing plenty that do, you're far less likely to find yourself eating fast-food and unhealthy snacks.

No matter what you do in the gym your body must have the nutrients it needs to grow. This is most important before and after you train because muscles break down during a workout. It is only during recovery that repair and growth can take place.
You need to eat after your workout. Right after a routine your body will try to convert sugar into

glycogen so your muscles can repair themselves and grow. If you don't eat after you exercise your body breaks down muscle into amino acids to convert into sugar.

After you work out eat a high-carbohydrate meal and add protein. For even greater results have a sports drink before and during exercise.

If you sleep for 6 to 8 hours and then skip breakfast your body will be running on fumes by the time you workout. This will send your body seeking sugar which, as we know, is easy to find. The most convenient foods are usually the same ones you should be avoiding. Skipping breakfast can lead to picking up bad habits like smoking or drinking, decreasing exercise and can cause you to follow fad diets. Common excuses for skipping breakfast are no time, not hungry, or dieting. Some people make a mistake by thinking that skipping breakfast means eating fewer calories which translates to weighing less but the body doesn't work like that. People who eat breakfast tend to take in more calories throughout the day but they also get more important nutrients than those who skip. Breakfast eaters also tended to consume less junk food and more fruits, vegetables and dairy. Breakfast eaters are less likely to be overweight. Eat breakfast every day for a fast way to fuel up first. I try and eat a package of instant oatmeal and mix in a scoop of whey protein powder, eggs, turkey sausage and blended fruit and veggies every morning.
Packing your lunch will keep your body satisfied and fed throughout the day without eating too much. You will also provide your body with what it needs for your workout no matter what time you exercise. This way you will be less likely to be tempted by the vending machine or hamburger stand. You will also save money if you eat only

what you bring. Diversify your food at every meal to get a combination of protein, carbohydrates and "good" fat. Make sure you add a little bit of protein into each snack.

The following foods should be added to your diet everyday:

• **Nuts** (not candy-covered, salted, or sprinkled over Ben and Jerry's...). Nuts are good for building muscle and fighting hunger. They contain: protein, monounsaturated fats, fiber and magnesium. This will fight against: obesity, heart disease, loss of muscle and cancer. There are "good" fats and "bad" fats just like "good" drugs and "bad" drugs. One is on your side to help you heal. The other fries your brain and makes you look stupid. Nuts contain monounsaturated fats, the good stuff that clears your arteries and fills you up. All nuts are high in this kind of fat and protein. The best nuts are raw almonds. Almonds are one of the best sources of vitamin E: a strong antioxidant that can help prevent cell damage after heavy workouts. Eat up to two handfuls a day. If you eat about 24 of them it can put off cravings. Don't buy them covered in chocolate or conveniently located inside a candy bar... Wash them down with water...

• **Beans** (not the refried ones from Taco Bell or the baked ones at a BBQ...) are good for building muscle, burning fat and helping "pass things along..." They contain: fiber, protein and iron. This will help fight against: obesity, colon cancer, heart disease and high blood pressure. Don't resist the beans because of some "bad" fat or that untimely gas. Beans are good for your heart and the more you eat them, the more you will be able to control your hunger.

• **Green Vegetables** (don't fry all the good stuff out of them or drown them in cheese) have Vitamins A, C, and K, beta-carotene, calcium, magnesium and fiber. They fight against: Cancer, heart disease, stroke, fat and bone loss. Our parents always tell us how important vegetables are for our health (They also said that cod liver oil is "not that bad"). Vegetables are also very important part of changing your diet. Popeye likes spinach because he could pop it up in the air, swallow it with one gulp and have instant muscles. You should eat it because one serving supplies nearly a full day of vitamin A and half of your vitamin C requirements. Its vitamins will protect you against heart disease, stroke and colon cancer. Broccoli is another one that is high in fiber and packed with more vitamins and minerals than almost any other food. If you hate vegetables as much as I do sneak them into other foods like pasta and in your juicer. Chop them into tiny pieces and add them to a sandwich so your body can absorb the nutrients.

• **Low-fat or fat-free milk, cheese, cottage cheese and yogurt** (once again, Ben and Jerry are not your friends and be easy on the cheese...) are good for building

a strong skeleton and speeding up weight loss. They fight against: bone loss, fat, high blood pressure and cancer. Low-fat yogurt, cheeses and other dairy products can play an important role in your diet. Milk or a milk substitute should be your major source of calcium. Liquids take up major room in your stomach which helps you fight hunger. Yogurt is a great combination of protein and carbohydrates for muscle recovery and growth

• **Oatmeal** (this can be rough on some people's taste buds but please don't load it with sugar...)

is great for boosting energy, reducing cholesterol and maintaining blood-sugar levels. It contains complex carbohydrates and fiber which fight against: heart disease, diabetes, colon cancer and fat. Oatmeal is the most important thing you can eat at breakfast. It will help you through sleepy mornings or to feel powerful by the time you workout in the morning. I use instant, low-sugar, steel-cut oatmeal for its convenience and quickness. If you absolutely must sweeten your oatmeal, use fruit, a small amount of honey, agave nectar or brown sugar. Oatmeal contains "sticky" fiber causing it to stay in your stomach longer than other fibers like vegetables. We all need more fiber. Fiber is like a bodyguard for your body keeping out heart disease and colon cancer. Studies have shown that oatmeal sustains your blood sugar levels longer than many other foods which keeps your insulin levels stable and helps you not be hungry for a few hours. This is important because when insulin is up your metabolism slows and your body stores fat. Since oatmeal breaks down so slowly in your stomach it causes less of a rise in insulin levels.

• **Eggs** (once again, try not to fry them in a bunch of salt, lard, cheese and bacon bits…) are great for building muscle and burning fat. They contain protein, vitamins A and B12 and fight against obesity. For a long time eggs were thought to be terrible because of their cholesterol content. You can cut out some of that by removing part of the yolk (the only tasty part) and eating the egg whites. The protein found in eggs has the highest value. This biological protein is the kind your body needs more than any food. The protein in eggs is more effective at building muscle than protein from milk and beef. You need less protein from eggs when you compare the calorie content than you do from other

sources including beef. This is why you will find a lot of egg-based protein powders. Eggs also contain vitamin B12 which is necessary for the breakdown of fat.

• **Turkey, lean steak, chicken and fish** (notice that our little Porky friend is not included?) are important for building muscle and improving your immune system. These meats contain: protein, iron, zinc, creatine, omega-3 fatty acids, vitamins B6 and B12, phosphorus and potassium. They fight against obesity and heart disease. Protein is the base of any solid diet plan to build muscle.

Turkey breast is one of the leanest meats. If you like dark meat it has lots of zinc and iron. Beef is another great muscle building protein. It is the best food source for creatine, the fuel for running your body's turbine engine when you are lifting weights.

One of the problems with beef is that unless it is lean it contains saturated fat. To cut down on the calories and get the most muscle for your buck (or steer in this case) look for meat cuts that are extra-lean like the "flat iron" and buy rounds or loins which are extra-lean. Sirloins and New York strips have less fat than prime ribs and T-bones… It's like a cow that is doing the workout with you: lean and tender!

Moving on to our swimming friends like tuna and salmon… These fish contain healthy doses of omega-3 fatty acids as well as protein. The omega-3 fatty acids and protein that salmon alone has swimming in it helps decrease muscle-protein breakdown after your workout and speeds up recovery. This is important, because in order to build new muscle you need to store new protein faster than your body breaks down the old stuff. Eating "Nemo" not your thing? That little oil your machine is missing cuts back your risks of heart disease, helps fight depression, protects against Alzheimer's and helps ease muscle soreness after workouts. Fortunately they are found in a bottle in vitamin form. You will NOT get the omega-3 fatty acids you need from the "You buy, we fry" catfish spot…

• **Peanut Butter** (watch out for the sugary ones…) is all-natural, sugar-free, cheap and convenient. It will boost your testosterone, build muscle and burn fat. Peanut Butter contains protein, monounsaturated fat and vitamin E and fights against: obesity, muscle loss and cardiovascular disease. The disadvantages of peanut butter are that it is high in calories and hard to find in restaurants! But it is full of that heart-healthy "good fat" that can increase your body's testosterone production. This will help your muscles grow and melt away fat.

• **Olive oil** (Grab a virgin…) When you achieve that "beach body" you might be tempted to rub this stuff all over you to get that 'bodybuilder look'. (Don't. You will fry up and resemble the color of fresh salmon…) You should however, eat the stuff. It is great in preventing muscle breakdown. Cook your food and toss your salads in this stuff and it will lower your cholesterol and boost your immune system. It contains 'good' fat and vitamin E. Olive oil fights against: Fat, cancer, heart disease and high blood pressure. Pass the bottle, enough said.

• **Whole-grain breads and cereals** (did I leave off doughnuts?? Yes- I did…) prevent your body from storing fat. They contain: fiber, protein, vitamin E, calcium, magnesium, potassium, zinc, and other great nutrients. Whole grains fight against: obesity, cancer, high blood pressure and heart disease.

• **Whey Protein Powder** (Soy is not better…) should be used for building muscle and burning fat. Picture a car with an engine that is constantly being repaired. That's what the inside of your body is like where the activities tear down and build up muscle tissue all day every day. After strength training, your body's mechanic wants to push the engine but it needs the right tools. That is why you must consume protein as soon as possible after workouts. Powdered whey protein is a type of animal protein that builds muscle. If you add whey powder to a fruit smoothie you can create one of the most powerful fat-burning meals possible. Whey protein consists of a high-quality protein that contains the amino acids you need to build muscle and burn fat. It is especially effective because it contains the highest amount of protein for the fewest number of calories. Finding one that cuts out the funky gas and tastes decent might take time, but will be well worth it.

• **Berries** protect your heart, can improve your eyesight and memory, and prevents hunger. They contain antioxidants, fiber, and vitamin C which fight against heart disease, cancer and obesity. Almost all berries are good for you (except Captain Crunch Berries…) They carry strong levels of antioxidants and help your body fight heart disease and cancer. Berries also help your eyesight, balance, coordination and short-term memory. Eat dark-red fruit to protect those muscles after a grueling workout. Red grapes, red cherries and pomegranates have antioxidants which can help reduce the inflammation that occurs in muscles after serious exercises.

HYDRATION (LUBRICATING THE MACHINE)

Caffeine is a drug that stimulates your central nervous system. Most energy drinks contain between 140 and 170 milligrams of caffeine in a 15- or 16-ounce can. The most caffeine-packed energy drink contains the equivalent in caffeine of about two 8-ounce cups of coffee. For some people this can cause headaches, sleeplessness or nausea.

Sugar is another ingredient you will often see on energy drink labels hidden in the word "Sucrose". It is a combination of fructose and glucose. Many energy drinks contain 50 to 60 grams of glucose or sucrose in a 16-ounce can. This can be a huge problem when you consume this much sugar on an empty stomach. This extra sugar causes your insulin levels to spike which tells your body to stop burning fat and start storing it. Sugary drinks like soda and energy drinks can trick your body with a blood-sugar rise which can make you skip other nutrient-rich foods you should be eating. If your daily sugar fix limits your muscles from getting amino acids it will drain the fuel you need for your workouts.

Your body runs mainly on glucose so adding more will give you an instant boost. Water and low-sugar sports drinks are what you should be drinking. Sugar can hide in products that we least expect. Be careful with dried fruits, certain nutrition bars and even ketchup. What is the deal with energy drinks? Most contain a high mixture of caffeine and sugar both which have been proven to increase performance. The problem is the extremely high amount of sugar in these drinks stops them from being a smart choice during exercise. There are other ingredients that offer stimulation often found in these drinks such as: guarana, ginseng and taurine which may also boost performance but can also increase your blood pressure and heart rate and make you feel "jittery" especially if taken on an empty stomach. Drink these only on a full stomach, well hydrated and looking to boost alertness and energy before or after a workout not during. Recovery drinks can significantly improve anyone's ability to have a quality workout the next day and the day after that.

As hard as our muscles appear they are approximately 80 percent water. When even a slight change of this percentage changes it can hinder exercise performance and slow recovery. The more dehydrated you are, the slower your body uses protein to build muscle. Drinking eight to 10 glasses of water a day and dividing 25 to 30 grams of your protein among five or six small meals throughout the day is ideal. This way you will put less stress on your kidneys and use more of the protein you are taking in by giving your body only as much as it can use each time. Try to drink at least 16 ounces of cold water as soon as you get up. This will boost your metabolism for the next hour and a half.

Dehydration due to exercise slows down your motor. It's like trying to make Usain Bolt sprint against his opponents while they are on a track and he is in a pool. You will feel exhausted sooner than you normally would. Knowing how much fluid you need to replace is an experiment at first. Losing sweat can range from a pint an hour to four times that amount and can also fluctuate due to the weather and clothing. If you try to drink when you are thirsty you probably are already dehydrated. Another way to measure dehydration is to check the color of your urine after a workout. If it is the color of a yellow highlight marker you're probably not drinking enough...

WARMING UP: PRIMING THE ENGINE

Most people think warming up means running on a treadmill, taking a lap or pedaling an exercise bike. That 10-minute aerobic workout only prepares the muscles in your legs to lift. A more efficient way to warm up is to do very light, quick reps using specific muscles you will be using in your weight workout. This will let your muscles know what you're about to ask them to do. That way you're prepared for high performance routines before you start. You must address each of the individual joints that you plan to exercise.

Warming up is what helps prevent injury by slowly increasing your blood flow and giving your muscles a chance to prepare for activity. You need to increase flexibility so it's in the normal range for example: touching your toes without bending your knees. By activating your muscle fibers you will improve your range of motion, so you can exert more force in your workout. Warming up this way will warm up your core temperature and increase your heart rate and blood flow. This warm-up will also make you stronger because applying stress to stretched-out muscles moving in different positions creates better flexibility. Your body will be more athletic and resistant to injury by the contraction and lengthening of your muscles.

DYNAMIC AND STATIC STRETCHING

Don't limit your stretching only when your muscles feel tight. Stretching the muscles you're working not only helps them stay loose but can also increase your range of motion allowing you to work more muscle fibers with each additional set.

There are two major types of stretching: dynamic and static.

A static stretch is exactly what it sounds like -- a movement in which you lean or pull until you feel a slight discomfort in the target muscle then stretching the muscle by holding that position for a specific number of seconds.

It is a common mistake to believe static stretching helps prevent injuries before a workout. This type of stretching causes the target muscle to relax, making it temporarily weaker which can cause imbalances in strength with its opposing muscle group. For example if you stretch your triceps it can cause them to become weaker than your biceps. This may make it more possible for you to strain, pull or tear a muscle. Never perform static stretching before you work out or play sports.

So is it ever good to do static stretches? Yes. These stretches are important for things we do everyday such as bending, kneeling and squatting. Stretching after a workout or game or any time of day except before an activity is great to improve flexibility. You will get the most gains by holding these stretches between 15 and 30 seconds.

A dynamic stretch is the opposite of a static stretch. In this stretch, your muscles move in and out of a stretched position constantly and fluidly. You need improvements in flexibility for sports and weight training because your muscles stretch at fast speeds in different body positions. Dynamic stretching is necessary for any workout program.

Dynamic stretching also increases blood flow, strength and power. It's a great warm-up for any activity. When you regularly perform both dynamic and static stretches some of the flexibility improvements from one will help the other. Dynamic and static stretching increases flexibility but most injuries occur within the normal range of motion. Stretching and warming up go together like peanut butter and jelly. Stretch when your muscles are already warm. It is important to spend twice as much time stretching your tight muscles as it is your flexible muscles. Work on your problem areas instead of your muscles that are already flexible. Most problem areas are hamstrings, shoulders and lower back muscles.

Champions aren't made
in the gyms.
CHAMPIONS
are made
from something they have deep inside them
-- a desire, a dream, a vision.

– Muhammad Ali

MONDAY

Dynamic Warm-up

1.   Jog 1 lap (400 meters) backwards

2.   Walking Lunges - 50 meters (Page 109)

3.   Diagonal Walking Lunges - 50 meters
      (Instead of lunging forward, lunge diagonally stretching your groin)

4.   High knee Jog - 50 meters

5.   Backward High Knee Jog - 50 meters

6.   Frogee Skips - 50 meters
      (Skip forward for 50 meters with each knee going straight out to the side. Return,
      skipping backwards for 50 meters with each knee going straight out to the side)

7.   Duck Walks - 50 meters
      (Squat down until your thighs are parallel to the ground. Stay in that position and   start
      walking, rotating your hips and keeping your feet under your butt)

8.   Balance Board Squats - 5 sets of 10 repetitions (Page 103)

9.   Rebound Jump squats – 20 repetitions (Page 99)

10.   Static Lunges - 20 repetitions (each leg) (Page 92)

11.   Jump lunges - 20 repetitions (Page 93)

12.   Donkeys – 30 repetitions (Page 83)

13.   Dirty Dogs - 30 repetitions (Page 84)

14.   Knee Circles - 30 repetitions (Page 83)
        (Combine exercises 12 and 13 making forward circles with your knee. Keep your
        right leg off of the ground for all of the repetitions. Repeat on the opposite leg)

15.   Reverse Knee Circles - 30 repetitions (Page 83)
        (Repeat exercise #14 now moving your knee in the opposite direction).

16.   Straight Leg Kicks – 30 repetitions (Page 85)

17.   Inside Mountain Climbers – 20 repetitions each leg (Page 148)
        (Perform with your feet landing inside of your hands)

18.   Outside Mountain Climbers – 20 repetitions (Page 148)
        (Perform with your feet landing outside of your hands)

19.   Frogees – 20 repetitions (Page 72)

Static Stretching

> "We are what we repeatedly do. Excellence, therefore,
> is not an act but a habit."
>
> **– Aristotle**

TUESDAY

Dynamic Warm-up

1.   Forward Push-up Crawl – 2 sets of 10 meters
        (Get in the push-up position. Maintaining this position, keeping your legs straight, walk
        forward using only your hands and feet)

2.   Backward Push-up Crawl – 2 sets of 10 meters
        (Get in the push-up position. Maintaining this position, keeping your legs straight,
        walk backward only using your hands and feet)

3.   Sideways Push-up Crawl – 2 sets of 10 meters
        (Get in the push-up position. Maintaining this position, keeping your legs straight,

walk sideways only using your hands and feet)

4. Forward Push-up Jumps – 2 sets of 10 meters
    (Get in the push-up position. Maintaining this position, keeping your legs straight,
    perform a push-up and explode forward only using your hands and feet)

5. Backward Push-up Jumps – 2 sets of 10 meters
    (Get in the push-up position. Maintaining this position, keeping your legs straight,
    perform a push-up and explode backward, only using your hands and feet)

6. Sideways Push-up Jumps – 2 sets of 10 meters
    (Get in the push-up position. Maintaining this position, keeping your legs straight,
    perform a push-up and explode sideways, only using your hands and feet)

7. Sports Ball Push-ups – 5 sets of 20 repetitions (Page 114)

8. Push-up Rows – 5 sets of 10 repetitions (Page 115)

9. Skull Crushers – 5 sets of 10 repetitions (Page 123)

Static Stretching

> "Pain is temporary. It may last a minute, or an hour, or a day, or a year,
> but eventually it will subside and something else will take its place.
> If I quit, however, it lasts forever."
>
> **– Lance Armstrong**

WEDNESDAY

Dynamic Warm-up

1. Rising Bridges - 3 sets of 1 minute (Page 69)
    (For 10 seconds while maintaining the bridge position, alternate raising each arm. Next,
    drive each knee toward your Elbow on that side for 10 seconds each. Finally, extend each
    foot out to the side as far as you can for 10 seconds each.)

2. Sky Divers - 3 sets of 10 repetitions (Page 82)

3. Swimmers – 3 sets of 10 repetitions (Page 81)

4. Mountain Climbers – 3 sets of 20 repetitions (Page 148)

5. Pendulums – 3 sets 20 repetitions each side (Page 74)

6. Frogees - 20 repetitions (Page 72)

7.   Side Twists – 3 sets of 20 repetitions each side (Page 67)

8.   Toe Reaches – 3 sets of 50 repetitions (Page 70)

9.   Bicycles – 3 sets of 30 repetitions (Page 75)

10.   "L"-shaped toe thrusts – 3 sets of 30 repetitions (Page 76)

Static Stretching

"You are never really playing an opponent.
You are playing yourself, your own highest standards,
and when you reach your limits, that is real joy"

– Arthur Ashe

THURSDAY

Dynamic Warm-up

1.   Reverse Push-ups - 5 sets of 10 repetitions (Page 138)

2.   Lawn Mower Starters – 5 sets of 10 repetitions (Page 139)

3.   Reverse Dumbbell Fly - 5 sets of 10 repetitions (Page 137)

4.   Shrugs - 5 sets of 10 repetitions (Page 129)

5.   Lat Pull-downs - 5 sets of 10 repetitions (Page 136)

Static Stretching

"You are never a loser until you quit trying"

-Mike Ditka

FRIDAY

Bike, Swim, Rowing, Surfing, Paddle boarding, Pilates, Yoga, Hiking, Recreational Sports, Martial Arts/Boxing, or Stretching

Hold yourself responsible
for a

HIGHER STANDARD

than anyone else
expects of you.
Never excuse yourself.

– Henry Ward Beecher

MONDAY

Dynamic Warm-up

1.   Squats on Balance Boards or Balance Discs - 5 sets of 10 repetitions (Page 103)

2.   Dumbbell Front Squats - 5 sets of 10 repetitions (Page 104)

3.   Lunges - 5 sets of 10 repetitions (Page 109)

4.   Straight-Leg Dead lifts – 5 sets of 10 repetitions (Page 106)

5.   Calf raises - 5 sets of 50 repetitions (Page 110)

Static Stretching

"Hard work spotlights the character of people:
some turn up their sleeves, some turn up their noses,
and some don't turn up at all"

-Sam Ewig

TUESDAY

Dynamic Warm-up

1.   Steering Wheels - 2 sets of 30 repetitions (Page 133)

2.   Shoulder Push-ups - 5 sets of 10 repetitions (Page 135)

3.   Forward Arm Circles - 2 sets of 20 repetitions (Page 134)

4. Reverse Arm Circles - 2 sets of 20 repetitions (Page 134)

5. Front Raises - 3 sets of 10 repetitions (Page 130)

6. Reverse-Grip Shoulder Press - 3 sets of 10 repetitions (Page 128)

"Without self-discipline success is impossible. Period"

- Lou Holtz

WEDNESDAY

Dynamic Warm-up

1. Swiss Ball Bridges - 3 sets of 1 minute (Page 69)
(Get into the bridge position, anchoring your feet on a bench and forearms on a Swiss ball)

2. Spiderman Bridges - 3 sets of 1 minute (Page 69)
(Alternate raising each knee to the outside of your elbow)

3. Tin Man Bridges - 3 sets of 1 minute (Page 69)
(Keeping your leg straight, alternate pushing each leg to the side, outside of your elbow)

4. Bicycles with Medicine Ball – 3 sets of 1 minute (Page 75)
(Perform while passing a medicine ball in-between your legs)

5. "L"-shaped toe thrusts – 3 sets of 1 minute (Page 76)

Static Stretching

"The harder you work, the harder it is to surrender"

-- Vince Lombardi

THURSDAY

Dynamic Warm-up

1. "T" Push-ups - 5 sets of 10 repetitions (Page 112)

2. Spiderman Push-ups – 5 sets of 10 repetitions (Page 111)

3.   1-hand Alternating Sports Ball Push-ups - 5 sets of 10 repetitions (Page 112)
(Perform a push-up with 1 hand on a medicine ball or basketball. While in the "Up" position roll the ball to the other hand and repeat)

4.   Lunging-Cable Chest Fly - 5 sets of 10 repetitions (Page 121)

5.   Double plate press - 5 sets of 10 repetitions (Page 120)

6.   Tricep Kick-outs - 5 sets of 10 repetitions (Page 122)

7.   Toe Busters - 3 sets of 30 seconds (Page 126)

Static Stretching

"In order to excel, you must be completely dedicated to your chosen sport.
You must also be prepared to work hard and be willing to accept destructive criticism.
Without 100 percent dedication, you won't be able to do this"

-Willie Mays

FRIDAY

Bike, Swim, Rowing, Surfing, Paddle boarding, Pilates, Yoga, Hiking, Recreational Sports, Martial Arts/Boxing, or Stretching

> **"**
> If you aren't
> # GOING ALL THE WAY,
> why go at all?
> **"**

-Joe Namath

MONDAY

Dynamic Warm-up

1. Sprint100 meters backwards and then perform 20 perfect push-ups (Page 116)

2. Sprint100 meters backwards and then perform 20 Ab-rollers (Page 77)

3. Sprint100 meters backwards and then perform 20 perfect push-ups

4. Sprint100 meters backwards and then perform 20 Ab-rollers

5. Sprint100 meters backwards and then lunge 100 meters (Page 109)

(Complete this circuit for twice)

Static Stretching

> "Even if you are on the right track,
> you'll get run over if you just sit there"

-- Will Rogers

TUESDAY

Dynamic Warm-up

1. 1-Arm Cable Pull-Downs - 5 sets of 10 repetitions (Page 141)

2. Reverse Push-ups - 5 sets of 10 repetitions (Page 138)

3. Reverse Dumbbell Fly - 5 sets of 10 repetitions (Page 137)

4.   Dumbbell Pull-overs on Swiss ball- 5 sets of 10 repetitions (Page 140)

5.   Lat Pull-downs - 5 sets of 10 repetitions (Page 136)

Static Stretching

"Success is not the results of spontaneous combustion.
You must set yourself on fire"

-Fred Shero

WEDNESDAY

Dynamic Warm-up

1.   Recliners - 5 sets of 30 repetitions (Page 78)

2.   Fish Out-of-Water - 5 sets of 30 repetitions (Page 79)

3.   Pendulums - 5 sets of 30 repetitions (Page 74)

4.   Oil Pumpers – 5 sets of 30 repetitions (Page 80)

5.   Worshipers – 5 sets of 30 repetitions (Page 68)

Static Stretching

"The winners in life treat their body as if it were a magnificent spacecraft
that gives them the finest transportation and endurance for their lives"

-Denis Waitley

THURSDAY

Dynamic Warm-up

1.   Decline-Spiderman Push-ups on a sports ball – 5 sets of 10 repetitions (Page 111)

2.   1-Hand Alternating Sports Ball Push-ups – 5 sets of 10 repetitions (Page 112)
(Perform a push-up with 1 hand on a medicine ball or basketball. While in the "Up" position roll the
ball to the other hand and repeat)

3.   Dumbbell Flys on Swiss Ball - 5 sets of 10 repetitions (Page 117)

4.   Dips - 5 sets of 10 repetitions (Page 119)

5.   Tricep Press-Down – 5 sets of 10 repetitions (Page 124)

Static Stretching

"If you are going to be a champion
you must be willing to pay a greater price"

-- Bud Wilkinson

FRIDAY

Bike, Swim, Rowing, Surfing, Paddle boarding, Pilates, Yoga, Hiking, Recreational Sports, Martial Arts/Boxing, or Stretching

"

If you train hard,

YOU'LL NOT ONLY BE HARD

you'll be hard to beat

"

-Herschel Walker

MONDAY

Dynamic Warm-up

1.   Backward-lunge knee drives - 3 sets of 10 repetitions (Page 94)

2.   Drop-catch squat - 3 sets of 10 repetitions (Page 96)

3.   Drop-under Squat - 3 sets of 10 repetitions (Page 97)

4.   Lunge strike - 3 sets of 10 repetitions (Page 98)

5.   Rebound-Jump Squats - 3 sets of 10 repetitions (Page 99)

6.   Overhead lunge matrix - 3 sets of 10 repetitions (Page 95)

7.   Medicine Ball Overhead Throw - 3 sets of 10 repetitions (Page 101)

8.   Medicine Ball Bucket Throw - 3 sets of 10 repetitions (Page 100)

Static Stretching

"Nothing ever comes to one that is worth having
except as a result of hard work"

-Booker T. Washington

TUESDAY

Dynamic Warm-up

1. Steering Wheels - 3 sets of 30 repetitions (Page 133)

2. Lateral Raises - 3 sets of 30 repetitions (Page 132)

3. Front Raises - 3 sets of 30 repetitions (Page 130)

4. Forward Arm Circles - 1 set of 60 seconds (Page 134)

5. Reverse Arm Circles - 1 set of 60 seconds (Page 134)

6. Backward Raises - 3 sets of 30 repetitions (Page 131)

7. Shrugs – 3 sets of 20 repetitions (Page 129)

8. Reverse Curls – 3 sets of 20 repetitions (Page 125)

9. Bicep Curls – 3 sets of 20 repetitions (Page 125)

10. Hammer Curls – 3 sets of 20 repetitions (Page 125)

Static Stretching

"It's a little like wrestling a gorilla.
You don't quit when you're tired,
you quit when the gorilla is tired"

-- Robert Strauss

WEDNESDAY

Dynamic Warm-up

1. Swimmers - 5 sets of 20 repetitions (Page 81)

2. Ab Rollers - 5 sets of 10 repetitions (Page 77)

3. Worshipers - 5 sets of 10 repetitions (Page 68)

4. Hanging Chairs – 5 sets of 1 minute (Page 71)

5. Recliners - 5 sets of 20 repetitions (Page 78)

6. Side Twists – 5 sets of 20 repetitions (Page 67)

Static Stretching

*"I've always made a total effort,
even when the odds seemed entirely against me.
never quit trying; I never felt that I didn't have a chance to win"*

-Arnold Palmer

THURSDAY

Dynamic Warm-up 2

1.   Reverse Push-ups - 5 sets of 10 repetitions (Page 138)

2.   Lawn Mower Starters – 5 sets of 10 repetitions (Page 139)

3.   Reverse Dumbbell Fly - 5 sets of 10 repetitions (Page 137)

4.   Shrugs - 5 sets of 10 repetitions (Page 129)

5.   Lat Pull-downs - 5 sets of 10 repetitions (Page 136)

Static Stretching

*"There is no happiness except in the realization
that we have accomplished something"*

-Henry Ford

FRIDAY

Bike, Swim, Rowing, Surfing, Paddle boarding, Pilates, Yoga, Hiking, Recreational Sports, Martial Arts/Boxing, or Stretching

> "
> You find that you have peace of mind and can enjoy yourself,
> get more sleep, rest when you know that it was a
>
> # ONE HUNDRED PERCENT EFFORT
>
> you gave - win or lose
> "

-Gordie Howe

MONDAY

Dynamic Warm-up

Find a stadium or park with at least 50 steps.

1.   Sprint up the steps, skipping a step as you reach 50 and walk down; Hop up every other step until you reach 50 and Spiderman (Page 142) down. 5 Sets

2.   Toe Taps - 1 set of 60 seconds (Sprint in place, tapping each foot on the step in front of you)

3.   1-Legged Hops - 1 set of 25 repetitions (Hop up the steps on your right leg up the 1st 25 steps then switch to the left for the next 25 steps)

4.   Falling Mummies – 1 set of 10 repetitions (Page 91)

5.   2 legged-hops – 1 set of 25 repetitions (Hop up every other step until you reach 50)

6.   Decline Push-ups – 1 set of 30 repetitions (Page 111) (Place your feet on a bench as you perform a pushup)

7.   Step Sprints – 1 set of 50 steps

8.   Squats – 1 set of 30 repetitions (Page 104) (Perform squats using just your body weight)

9.   Spidermans – 1 set of 50 steps (Page 142)

Static Stretching

"There are only two options regarding commitment; you're either in or you're out. There's no such thing as life in-between"

-Pat Riley

TUESDAY

Dynamic Warm-up

1.   Swiss Ball Push-ups – 5 sets of 20 repetitions (Page 114)

2.   Incline Swiss Dumbbell press 5 sets of 10 repetitions (Page 118)

3.   Lunging-Cable Chest fly – 5 sets of 10 repetitions (Page 121)

4.   Double-Plate Chest Press – 5 sets of 10 repetitions (Page 120)

5.   Skull Crushers – 5 sets of 10 repetitions (Page 123)

Static Stretching

"Pressure is a word that is misused in our vocabulary. When you start thinking of pressure, it's because you've started to think of failure"

-Tommy Lasorda

WEDNESDAY

Dynamic Warm-up

1.   Toe Reaches – 5 sets of 20 repetitions (Page 70)

2.   Recliners – 5 sets of 20 repetitions (Page 78)

3.   Side Twists – 5 sets of 20 repetitions each side (Page 67)

4.   Oil Pumpers – 5 sets of 20 repetitions each side (Page 80)

5.   Abdominal Crunches – 5 sets of 50 (Page 66)

Static Stretching

"Nobody who ever gave his best regretted it"

-George Halas

THURSDAY

Dynamic Warm-up

1.   1000 Jump ropes
2.   Twenty-Ones - 3 sets of 21 repetitions (Page 125) (Hold a curl bar with an underhand grip and let it hang in front of your waist. Curl the bar up to the bottom of your chest 7 times. On the 7th repetition, curl the bar to your shoulders. Next, perform 7 curls from the bottom of your chest up to your shoulders. Lastly, perform 7 full curls from the front of your waist up to your shoulders)

3.   Hammer Curls - 3 sets of 10 repetitions (Page 125)

4.   Reverse curls - 3 sets of 10 repetitions (Page 125)

5.   Toe Busters – 3 sets of 30 seconds (Page 126)

Static Stretching

"The only way of finding the limits of the possible
is by going beyond them into the impossible"

-Arthur C. Clarke

FRIDAY

Bike, Swim, Rowing, Surfing, Paddle boarding, Pilates, Yoga, Hiking, Recreational Sports, Martial Arts/Boxing, or Stretching

I WORK HARD EVERY DAY

MONDAY

Dynamic Warm-up

1.   Hurdle Walkovers - 3 sets of 6 hurdles (Page 89)

2.   Hurdle-Hip Mobility – 5 sets of 3 hurdles (Page 87)

3.   Hurdle Straight-leg Side Skips - 3 sets of 6 hurdles (Page 88)

4.   Hurdle-Heel Crossovers - 3 sets of 30 repetitions (Page 86)

These exercises are performed on a hockey slide board:

5.   Long Slides - 3 sets of 30 repetitions (Page 150) (Perform 30 slides on the slide board with re-sistance bands around your ankles. Returning to the starting side is one repetition)

6.   Mountain Climbers - 3 sets of 30 repetitions (Page 148) (Perform with your hands on the slide board with resistance bands around your ankles)

7.   Frogees - 3 sets of 30 repetitions (Page 72)

8.   Leg Curl Slides - 3 sets of 30 repetitions (Page151)

9.   Windshield Wiper Slides - 3 sets of 30 repetitions (Page 149) (Perform 30 repetitions on the slide board with resistance bands around your ankle)

Static Stretching

"If your actions inspire others to dream more, learn more, do more and become more, you are a leader"

-John Quincy Adams

TUESDAY

Dynamic Warm-up

1.   Spidermans – 5 sets of 50 steps (Page 142)

2.   Lateral Raises – 5 sets of 10 repetitions (Page 132)

3.   Front Raises - 5 sets of 10 repetitions (Page 130)

4.   Shrugs - 5 sets of 10 repetitions (Page 129)

5.   Reverse Curls - 5 sets of 10 repetitions (Page 125)

6.   Toe Busters - 5 sets of 30 seconds (Page 126)

Static Stretching

"Today, you have 100 percent of your life left"

-Tom Landry

WEDNESDAY

Dynamic Warm-up

1.   Bridges - 3 sets of 2 minutes (Page 69)

2.   Mountain Climbers – 3 set of 1 minute (Page 148)

3.   Frogees – 3 set of 1 minute (Page 72)

4.   Fish Out-of-Water – 3 set of 30 each side (Page 79)

5.   Worshippers - 3 sets of 20 repetitions (Page 68)

6.   Ab Rollers - 3 sets of 10 repetitions (Page 77)

Static Stretching

"There is only one way to succeed at anything and that is to give everything"

-Vince Lombardi

THURSDAY

Dynamic Warm-up

1. 1-Arm Cable Pull-Downs - 5 sets of 10 repetitions (Page 141)

2. Reverse Push-ups - 5 sets of 10 repetitions (Page 138)

3. Reverse Dumbbell Fly - 5 sets of 10 repetitions (Page 137)

4. Dumbbell Pull-overs on Swiss ball- 5 sets of 10 repetitions (Page 140)

5. Lat Pull-downs - 5 sets of 10 repetitions (Page 136)

Static Stretching

"Hard work beats talent when talent doesn't work hard"

-Tim Notke

FRIDAY

Bike, Swim, Rowing, Surfing, Paddle boarding, Pilates, Yoga, Hiking, Recreational Sports, Martial Arts/Boxing, or Stretching

"
A man is
NOT FINISHED
when he is defeated. He is finished when he quits
"

-Richard Nixon

MONDAY

Dynamic Warm-up

1.   Box Hops- 5 sets of 10 repetitions (Page 143)

2.   Deadlifts – 5 sets of 10 repetitions (Page 107)

3.   1-Foot Box Hops - 5 sets of 10 repetitions each leg (Page 143) (With a dumbbell in each hand jump on top of an 18 inch box with your left leg while simultaneously curling the dumbbells to your shoulders with a hammer grip (Page 125). Step down and repeat with right leg)

4.   Lunges - 5 sets of 10 repetitions each leg (Page 109)

5.   Step-ups - 5 sets of 10 repetitions each leg (Page 108)

6.   Calf Raises - 5 sets of 50 repetitions (Page 110)

Static Stretching

"The difference between a successful person and others
is not a lack of strength, not a lack of knowledge,
but rather a lack of will"

-Vince Lombardi

TUESDAY

Dynamic Warm-up

1.   Swiss ball push-ups - 5 sets of 20 repetitions (Page 114) (Perform with your hands on a Swiss ball)

2.   Swiss ball alternating dumbbell press, dumbbell press and fly – 5 sets of 10 repetitions each exercise (Pages 118 and 117) (Lying on a Swiss ball, perform the dumbbell press 1 arm at a time (10 times each arm) while the opposite arm is straight up holding the weight. Without pausing, perform 10 dumbbell presses with both arms going up simultaneously. For the last portion of the set, perform 10 flys)

3.   Dips - 5 sets of 10 repetitions (Page 119)

4.   Tricep Kick-outs - 5 sets of 10 repetitions (Page 122)

Static Stretching

*"If you don't have time to do it right,
when will you have time to do it over?"*

-John Wooden

WEDNESDAY

Dynamic Warm-up

1.   Swiss Ball Bridges - 5 sets of 1 minute (Page 69) (Get into the bridge position but anchor your feet on a bench and forearms on a Swiss ball)

2.   Spiderman Bridges - 5 sets of 1 minute (Page 69) (Alternate raising each knee to the outside of your elbow)

3.   Tin Man Bridges - 5 sets of 1 minute (Page 69) (Keeping your legs straight, alternate pushing each leg to the side, outside of your elbow)

4.   Bicycles with Medicine Ball – 5 sets of 1 minute (Page 75) (Perform while passing a medicine ball in-between your legs)

5.   "L"-shaped toe thrusts – 5 sets of 1 minute (Page 76)

Static Stretching

*"Happy are those who dream dreams
and are ready to pay the price to make them come true"*

-Leon J. Suenes

THURSDAY

Dynamic Warm-up

1.   Reverse Push-ups - 5 sets of 10 repetitions (Page 138)

2.   Lawn Mower Starters – 5 sets of 10 repetitions (Page 139)

3.   Reverse Dumbbell Fly - 5 sets of 10 repetitions (Page 137)

4.   Shrugs - 5 sets of 10 repetitions (Page 129)

5.   Lat Pull-downs - 5 sets of 10 repetitions (Page 136)

Static Stretching

"Develop the winning edge;
small differences in your performance
can lead to large differences in your results"

-- Brian Tracy

FRIDAY

Bike, Swim, Rowing, Surfing, Paddle boarding, Pilates, Yoga, Hiking, Recreational Sports, Martial Arts/Boxing, or Stretching

> ""
> Things may come to those who wait,
> but only the things left by

THOSE WHO HUSTLE

> ""

-Abraham Lincoln

MONDAY

Dynamic Warm-up

Find a stadium with at least 50 steps.

1.   Umbrellas with calf raises - 10 sets (Page 144 and Page 110) (At the bottom, perform 25 calf raises holding the weight at your chest, standing on a step with the balls of your feet.)

2.   Squats - 5 sets of 10 repetitions (Page 104) (Hold the plate or medicine ball at chest level with your arms extended)

3.   Lunges - 5 sets of 10 repetitions (Page 109) (Hold the plate or medicine ball at chest level)

Static Stretching

> "I learned that if you want to make it bad enough,
> no matter how bad it is,
> you can make it"
>
> **-- Gale Sayers**

TUESDAY

Dynamic Warm-up

1.   Perfect push-ups - 5 sets of 10 repetitions (Page 116)

2.   Balance board push-ups - 5 sets of 10 repetitions (Page 113)

3.   Swiss-ball push-ups - 5 sets of 10 repetitions (Page 114)

4.   Sports ball push-ups - 5 sets of 10 repetitions (Page 114)

5.   Push-up Rows – 5 sets of 10 repetitions (Page 115)

6.   1-Hand Alternating Sports Ball Push-ups - 5 sets of 10 repetitions (Page 112)
(Perform a push-up with 1 hand on a medicine ball or basketball. While in the "Up" position roll the ball to the other hand and repeat)

7.   Double-plate press - 5 sets of 10 repetitions (Page 120)

8.   Tricep Press-Down - 5 sets of 10 repetitions (Page 124)

Static Stretching

*"What would life be
if we had no courage to attempt anything?"*

-Vincent van Gogh

WEDNESDAY

Dynamic Warm-up

1.   Abdominal Crunches – 250 total repetitions (Page 66) (Perform as many crunches as possible per set until you reach 250, holding a weight or medicine ball with your arms outstretched)

2.   Toe Reaches – 100 total repetitions (Page 70) (Perform as many reaches per set as possible until you reach 100, holding a weight or medicine ball with your arms outstretched)

3.   Bicycles – 200 total repetitions (Page 75) (Perform as many bicycles per set as possible until you reach 200)

4.   "L"-shaped toe thrusts - 100 total repetitions (Page 76) (Perform as many thrusts as possible per set until you reach 100)

5.   Bridges - 5 total minutes (Page 69) (Perform bridges as long as possible until you reach 5 minutes total)

Static Stretching

*"Don't measure yourself by what you have accomplished,
but by what you should accomplish
with your ability"*

-John Wooden

THURSDAY

Dynamic Warm-up

1.   Shoulder Push-ups - 5 sets of 10 repetitions (Page 135)

2.   Reverse-grip shoulder press- 5 sets of 10 repetitions (Page 128)

3.   Beggars - 5 sets of 10 repetitions (Page 127)

4.   Shrugs - 5 sets of 10 repetitions (Page 129)

5.   Hammer Curls - 5 sets of 10 repetitions (Page 125)

6.   Bicep Curls - 5 sets of 10 repetitions (Page 125)

Static Stretching

"There are no gains without pains"

-Adlai Stevenson

FRIDAY

Bike, Swim, Rowing, Surfing, Paddle boarding, Pilates, Yoga, Hiking, Recreational Sports, Martial Arts/Boxing, or Stretching

"
ALWAYS DO
what you are afraid to do

"

-Ralph Waldo Emerson

MONDAY

Dynamic Warm-up

1.   Balance Board Squats - 5 sets of 10 repetitions (Page 103)

2.   Squatting Mummies - 5 sets of 10 repetitions (Page 90)

3.   Falling Mummies - 5 sets of 10 repetitions (Page 91)

4.   Deadlifts - 5 sets of 10 repetitions (Page 107)

5.   Calf Raises- 5 sets of 50 repetitions (Page 110)

Static Stretching

> "The more I want to get something done,
> the less I call it work"
>
> **-Richard Bach**

TUESDAY

Dynamic Warm-up

1.   1-Arm Cable Pull-Downs - 5 sets of 10 repetitions (Page 141)

2.   Reverse Push-ups - 5 sets of 10 repetitions (Page 138)

3.   Reverse Dumbbell Fly - 5 sets of 10 repetitions (Page 137)

4.   Dumbbell Pull-overs on Swiss ball- 5 sets of 10 repetitions (Page 140)

WEEK 9

5.   Lat Pull-downs - 5 sets of 10 repetitions (Page 136)

Static Stretching

> "Courage is not the absence of fear,
> but simply moving on with dignity
> despite that fear"
>
> **-Pat Riley**

WEDNESDAY

Dynamic Warm-up

1.   Recliners - 5 sets of 20 (Page 78)

2.   Fish Out-of-Water - 5 sets of 1 minute (Page 79)

3.   Bicycles - 5 sets of 1 minute (Page 75)

4.   Pendulums – 5 sets of 30 repetitions (each side) (Page 74)

5.   Oil Pumpers – 5 sets of 30 repetitions (each side) (Page 80)

Static Stretching

> "To succeed...
> You need to find something to hold on to,
> something to motivate you,
> something to inspire you"
>
> **-- Tony Dorsett**

THURSDAY

Dynamic Warm-up

1.   Mogul Twist Squat Jumps – 3 sets of 10 repetitions (each side) (Page 102)

2.   Lunge Strike – 3 sets of 10 repetitions (each leg) (Page 98)

3.   Static Lunge – 3 sets of 10 repetitions (each leg) (Page 92)

4.   Straight-leg Dead lift– 3 sets of 10 repetitions (Page 106)

5. Lunging-cable chest fly – 3 sets of 10 repetitions (Page 121)

6. Deadlift with Shrug – 3 sets of 10 repetitions (Page 107) and (Page 129)

7. Drop-Under Squats – 3 sets of 10 repetitions (Page 97)

8. Rebound-Jump Squats – 3 sets of 10 repetitions (Page 99)

Static Stretching

"You must do the very thing
you think you cannot do"

-Eleanor Roosevelt

FRIDAY

Bike, Swim, Rowing, Surfing, Paddle boarding, Pilates, Yoga, Hiking, Recreational Sports, Martial Arts/Boxing, or Stretching

> ❝
> Success is the
> # SUM OF
> # SMALL EFFORTS
> repeated day in and day out
> ❞

-Robert Collier

MONDAY

Dynamic Warm-up

1.   400 meter backward run

2.   Sled Sprints – 2 sets of 50 meters (Page 146) (Load a sled with weights and attach a harness to it. Sprint for 50 meters. Staying low to the ground and backpedal the sled back to the starting position)

3.   Parachute Sprints – 2 sets of 50 meters (Page 145) (Attach a harness to a parachute and sprint for 50 meters)

4.   Bungee Sprints – 2 sets of 10 repetitions (Page 147) (Attach a harness to a bungee cord and sprint to a cone 10 meters away. Walk carefully backward to the starting position and repeat)

Static Stretching

> "Face your deficiencies and acknowledge them.
> But do not let them master you"
>
> **-- Hellen Keller**

TUESDAY

Dynamic Warm-up

1.   Perfect Push-ups – 3 sets of 20 repetitions (Page 116) (for a advanced move perform with your feet elevated)

2.	Balance Board Push-ups – 3 sets of 20 repetitions (Page 113) (for a advanced move perform with your feet elevated)

3.	Sports Ball Push-ups – 3 sets of 20 repetitions (Page 114) (for a advanced move perform with your feet elevated)

4.	Tricep Kick-outs – 5 sets of 10 repetitions (Page 122)

Static Stretching

"The most important key to achieving great success
is to decide upon your goal
and launch, get started, take action, move"

-John Wooden

WEDNESDAY

Dynamic Warm-up

1.	Mountain climbers on Ab Roller – 5 sets of 1 minute (Page 73)

2.	Bridges – 5 sets of 1 minute (Page 69)

3.	Ab Roller – 5 sets of 1 minute (Page 77)

4.	Abdominal Crunches – 5 sets of 1 minute (Page 66)

Static Stretching

"Adversity causes some men to break;
others to break records"

-- William A. Ward

THURSDAY

Dynamic Warm-up

1.	Steering Wheels - 50 repetitions total (Page 133)

2.	Beggars - 50 repetitions total (Page 127)

3.   Lateral raises - 50 repetitions total (Page 132)

4.   Backward raises - 50 repetitions total (Page 131)

5.   Shrugs - 50 repetitions total (Page 129)

6.   Reverse Curls - 50 repetitions total (Page 125)

7.   Toe Busters – 3 minutes total (Page 126)

Static Stretching

"Life can be pulled by goals
just as surely as it can be pushed by drives"

-Viktor Frankl

FRIDAY

Bike, Swim, Rowing, Surfing, Paddle boarding, Pilates, Yoga, Hiking, Recreational Sports, Martial Arts/Boxing, or Stretching

Every game is an

OPPORTUNITY

to measure yourself against your own potential

-- Bud Wilkinson

MONDAY

Dynamic Warm-up

Find a stadium with at least 50 steps.

1.   Sprint up the steps, skipping a step as you reach 50 and walk down - 5 Sets

2.   Hop up every other step until you reach 50, then Spiderman (Page 142) down - 5 Sets

3.   Mogul Twist-Squat Jumps – 3 sets of 10 repetitions (Page 102)

4.   Deadlifts – 3 sets of 10 repetitions (Page 107)

5.   Straight-leg Deadlifts – 3 sets of 10 repetitions (Page 106)

Static Stretching

"Sometimes it is more important to discover what one cannot do than what one can do"

-- Lin Yutang

TUESDAY

Dynamic Warm-up

1.   "T" push-ups - 50 repetitions total (Page112)

2.   Push-up rows - 50 repetitions total (Page 115)

3.   Dumbbell Fly - 50 repetitions total (Page 117)

4.   Dips - 50 repetitions total (Page 119)

5.   Skull Crushers - 50 repetitions total (Page 123)

Static Stretching

> "I've had smarter people around me all my life,
> but I haven't run into one yet that can outwork me.
> And if they can't outwork you, then smarts aren't going to do them much good.
> That's just the way it is. And if you believe that and live by it,
> you'd be surprised at how much fun you can have"
>
> **-Woody Hayes**

WEDNESDAY

Dynamic Warm-up

1.   Hanging Chairs – 5 sets of 1 minute (Page 71)

2.   Abdominal Crunches – 5 sets of 20 repetitions (Page 66)

3.   Side Twists - 5 sets of 20 repetitions (Page 67)

4.   Toe Reaches – 5 sets of 20 repetitions (Page 70)

5.   Recliners – 5 sets of 20 repetitions (Page 78)

6.   Bicycles – 5 sets of 20 repetitions (Page 75) (Pass a medicine ball between your legs in each rotation)

Static Stretching

> "If you don't know where you are going,
> you'll end up someplace else"
>
> **-Yogi Berra**

THURSDAY

Dynamic Warm-up

1. Balance Board Squats – 30 repetitions (Page 103)

2. Rebound-Jump Squats – 30 repetitions (Page 99)

3. Jump lunges – 30 repetitions (Page 93)

4. Static Lunges – 30 repetitions (each leg) (Page 92)

5. Donkeys – 30 repetitions (Page 83)

6. Dirty Dogs - 30 repetitions (Page 84)

7. Knee Circles - 30 repetitions (Page 83)
(Combine exercises 5 and 6 making forward circles with your knee. Keep your right leg off of the ground for all of the repetitions. Repeat on the opposite leg)

8. Straight Leg Kicks – 30 repetitions (Page 85)

9. Calf raises – 5 sets of 50 repetitions (Page 110)

Static Stretching

"Only those who dare to fail greatly
can ever achieve greatly"

- Robert F. Kennedy

FRIDAY

Bike, Swim, Rowing, Surfing, Paddle boarding, Pilates, Yoga, Hiking, Recreational Sports, Martial Arts/Boxing, or Stretching

The undertaking of a

NEW ACTION

brings new strength

-Richard L. Evans

MONDAY

Dynamic Warm-up

1. Step-ups - 50 repetitions total (Page 108) (use a weight that is heavy as you can hold)

2. Drop-under Squats – 5 sets of 10 repetitions (Page 97)

3. Calf Raises – 5 sets of 20 repetitions (Page 110) (hold the weight used from exercise #2 at chest level)

Static Stretching

"Nobody is stronger, nobody is weaker than someone who came back.
There is nothing you can do to such a person because whatever you could do
is less than what has already been done to him.
We have already paid the price"

- Elie Wiesel

TUESDAY

Dynamic Warm-up

1. 1-Arm Cable Pull-Downs - 5 sets of 10 repetitions (Page 141)

2. Reverse Push-ups - 5 sets of 10 repetitions (Page 138)

3. Reverse Dumbbell Fly - 5 sets of 10 repetitions (Page 137)

4.   Dumbbell Pullovers on Swiss ball- 5 sets of 10 repetitions (Page 140)

5.   Lat Pull-downs - 5 sets of 10 repetitions (Page 136)

Static Stretching

"Start off everyday with a smile and get it over with"

-W.C. Fields

WEDNESDAY

Dynamic Warm-up

1.   Rising Bridges - 3 sets of 1 minute (Page 69)

2.   Sky Divers - 3 sets of 10 repetitions (Page 82)

3.   Mountain Climbers (hands landing inside your feet) – 20 repetitions (Page 148)

4.   Mountain Climbers (hands landing outside your feet) – 20 repetitions each leg (Page 148)

5.   Pendulums – 3 sets 20 repetitions each side (Page 74)

6.   Frogees - 20 repetitions (Page 72)

7.   Side Twists – 3 sets of 20 repetitions each side (Page 67)

8.   Toe Reaches – 3 sets of 50 repetitions (Page 70)

9.   Bicycles – 3 sets of 30 repetitions (Page 75)

10. "L"-shaped toe thrusts – 3 sets of 30 repetitions (Page 76)

Static Stretching

"We must embrace pain and burn it as fuel for our journey"

- Miyazawa Kenji

THURSDAY

Dynamic Warm-up

1. Steering Wheels - 2 sets of 30 repetitions (Page 133)

2. Shoulder Push-ups - 5 sets of 10 repetitions (Page 135)

3. Forward Arm Circles - 2 sets of 20 repetitions (Page 134)

4. Reverse Arm Circles - 2 sets of 20 repetitions (Page 134)

5. Front Raises - 3 sets of 10 repetitions (Page 130)

6. Reverse-Grip Shoulder Press - 3 sets of 10 repetitions (Page 128)

7. Hammer Curls - 3 sets of 10 repetitions (Page 125)

8. Bicep Curls - 3 sets of 10 repetitions (Page 125)

9. Toe Busters - 3 sets of 30 seconds (Page 126)

Static Stretching

"Once you say you're going to settle for second,
that's what happens to you in life"

- John F. Kennedy

FRIDAY

Bike, Swim, Rowing, Surfing, Paddle boarding, Pilates, Yoga, Hiking, Recreational Sports, Martial Arts/Boxing, or Stretching

ABDOMINAL CRUNCHES

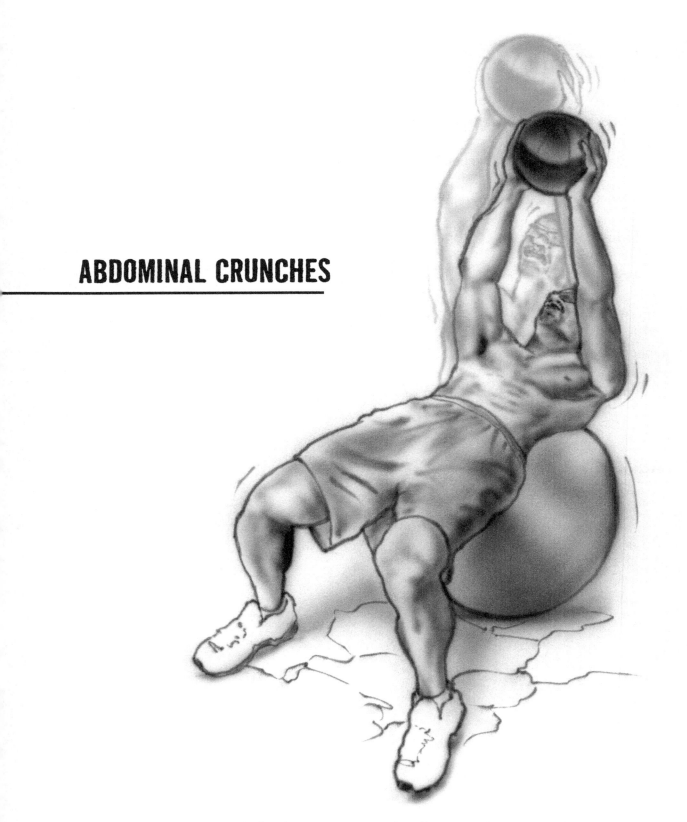

Start by sitting on a Swiss ball or bench with your feet flat. Your lower back should be in contact with ball or bench. Holding a weight over your chest with your arms extended, curl your shoulders toward your pelvis without lifting your lower back from the surface of the ball or bench.

Exhale with force at the top of the movement when you do abdominal crunches. This will force your abs to work harder.

SIDE TWISTS

Stand with feet shoulder width apart and knees slightly bent. Hold a weight away from your chest and rotate your upper body to the left side and then all the way back around to the right without moving your arms. This exercise will help you build your shoulders and obliques, the muscles that are hiding underneath our "love handles". Obliques are like the 'spotlights' for our abs. They make them stand out while protecting them also. Do not rotate too quickly or forcefully so that you do not put your spine under stress.

WORSHIPERS

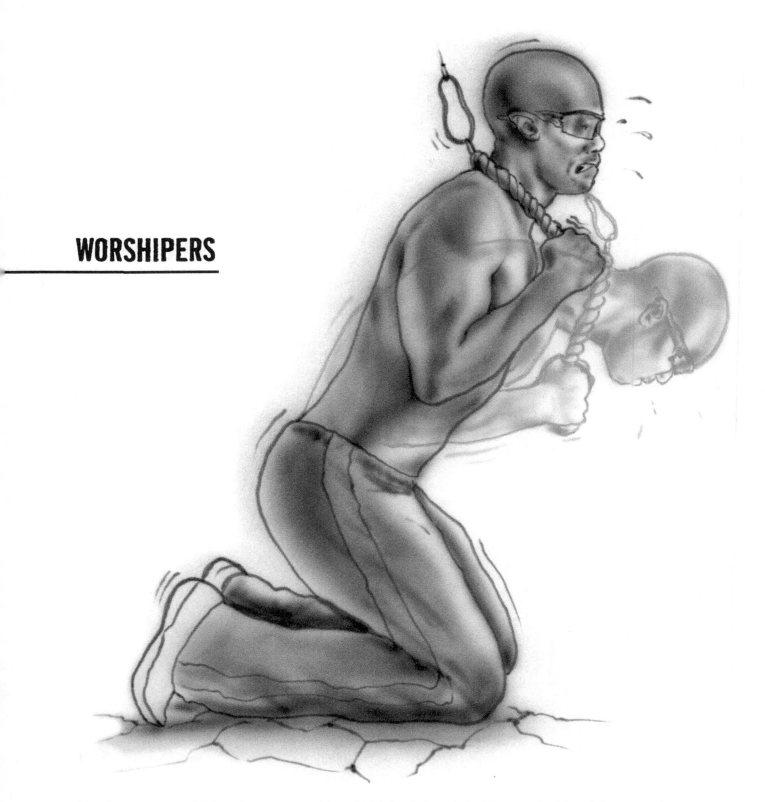

Attach a rope to a high point on the cables. With both hands holding each side of the rope close to your cheeks, bend forward pulling your elbows toward your hips. Keep the rope in the same position the entire time. Return to the starting position. This exercise can be done with your back against the pulley machine or facing it. Worshipers train your body to resist forces (especially the evil ones...) and resistance is one of the most important functions of your core..

RISING BRIDGES

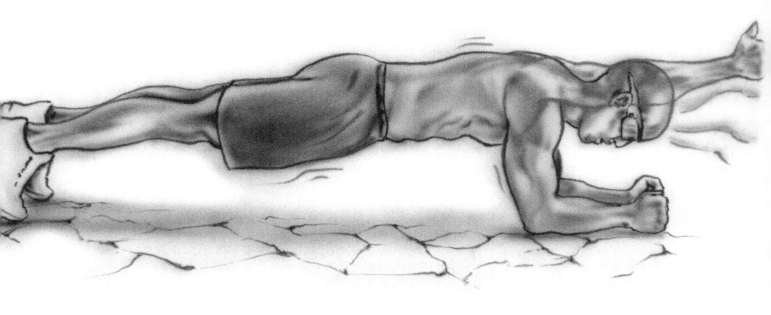

Get into a pushup position but rest your weight on your forearms instead of your hands. Your elbows should be directly underneath your shoulders. By lifting one arm or one leg in the air you force your core to work even harder to fight your body from twisting to one side. The bridge is a body-weight exercise that works the abs and hip flexors, glutes and lats. Side bridges improve the stability of all the muscles surrounding your spine and stomach.

TOE REACHES

Lying on your back and extend your legs straight up in the air with your feet pointing down toward your stomach. Reach a weight toward your toes keeping your lower back on the ground. Return to the starting position. Try to keep your legs completely straight and your lower back on the ground. Your feet should be directly over your hips. Drawing your legs toward your abs works the lower portion of your abs.

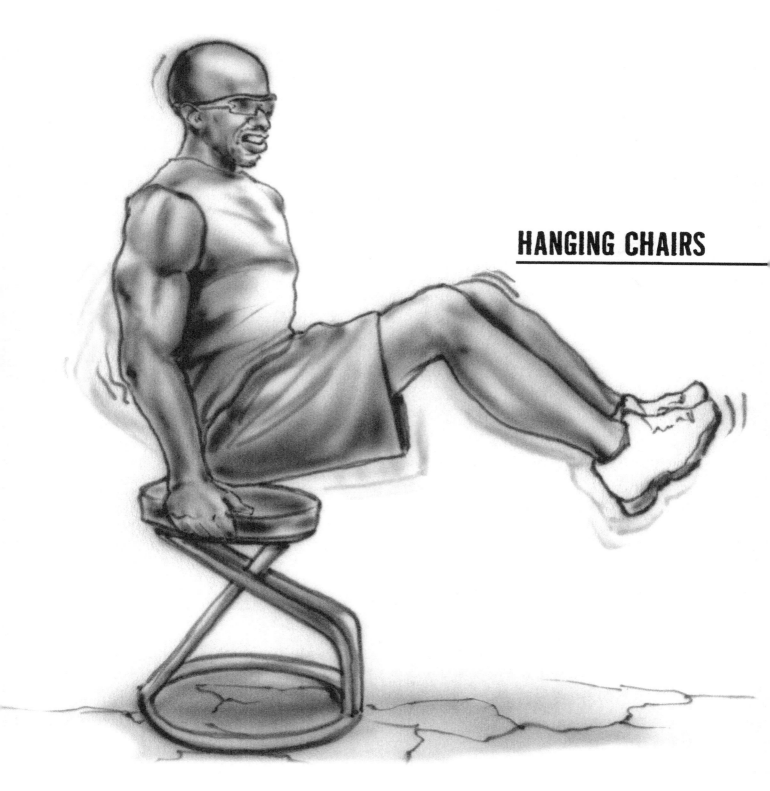

HANGING CHAIRS

Hold yourself up on your hands with your arms straight on a bench with your knees tucked up to your chest. When you do hanging knee chairs, round out your back by rolling your pelvis and hips toward your chest instead of just raising your legs. This way you will not just work the muscles at the top of your thighs

FROGEES

Get in the push-up position. Thrust hips forward allowing your feet to land just outside of your hands. Thrust your hips backward to return to the starting position. Frogees strengthens the lower back, hips, and groin muscles. When people call me 'Kermit the Frog', I take it as a complement…

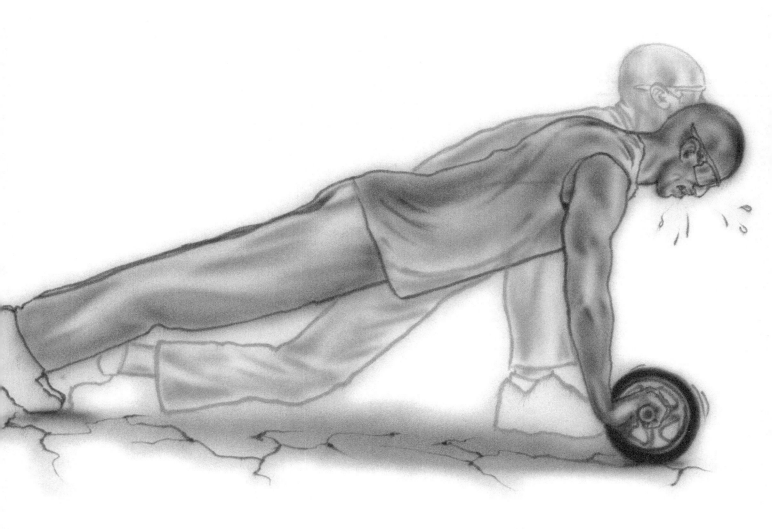

MOUNTAIN CLIMBERS

This variation of the Mountain Climber is done slowly and under control. Get in the pushup position. Place your hands on the ground, a medicine ball or ab-roller. Lift your left foot off the floor and bring your left knee forward as close to your elbow as possible, keeping your back in a straight line. Return to the starting position, and repeat with your right leg. This strengthens your abs, lower back, and hips. It also stabilizes the joints around the shoulder.

PENDULUMS

Stand with your knees slightly bent and your legs shoulder-width apart. Hold a plate or a pair of dumbbells directly over you head with your elbows slightly bent. Bend to your left side as far as possible without twisting your lower body and then bend to the right side as far as possible. Pendulums help you lose that 'muffin top' and trade them in for well-defined external and internal obliques, the sides of your abs that protect your abs and spine.

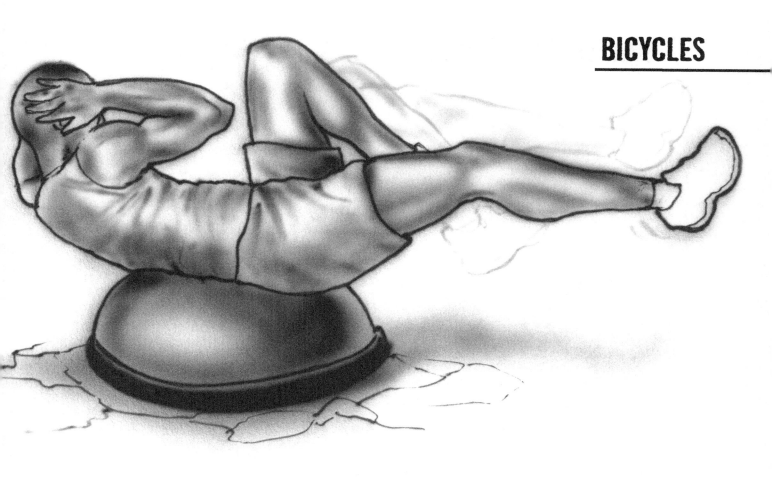

BICYCLES

Lie on your back on the floor or a Swiss ball with your right knee bent at 90 degrees and your left leg extended with your hands behind your head. Pedal your legs like you are on a bike, touching each elbow to the opposite knee without letting your heel touch the ground. Returning to the starting side = 1 repetition. This old-school exercise works the obliques and your entire six-pack without the worry of a flat tire or having to stay in the bike lane.

"L" SHAPED TOE THRUSTS

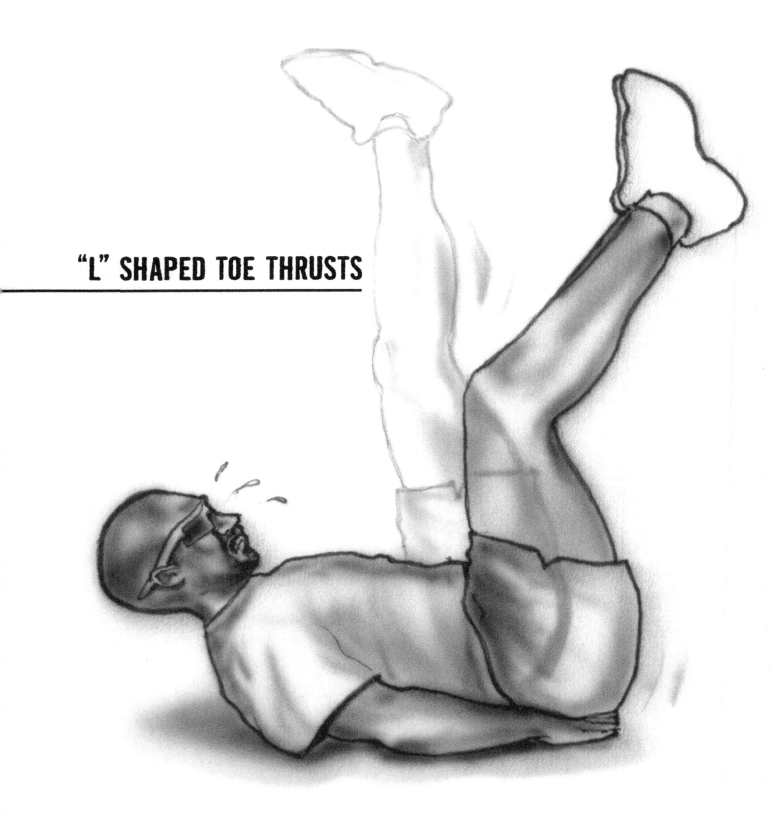

Lie on your back and extend your legs straight up over your hips. Place your arms flat on the ground beside you with your palms down. Thrust your feet toward the ceiling using your lower abs keeping you hips off of the ground. Return to the starting position. Keep your abs contracted without arching your back. This strengthens your abs and hip flexors.

AB ROLLERS

While on your knees, roll the ab roller out as far as you can without letting your hips sag or arching your back. As your strength increases you will be able to go until your torso is parallel to the ground. Reverse the movement using your abs to return to the starting position, keeping your butt and core tight throughout the exercise. You can also perform this exercise by using a barbell and two 10-pound weight plates. Ab rollers will force your abs to contract in order to keep your body stable.

RECLINERS

In a seated position with your torso reclining 45 degrees, hold a weight out in front of you with your arms extended. Twist your torso from side to side, tapping the weight on each side of the ground while keeping your feet 6 inches off of the ground and your heels touching each other. Recliners strengthen both the upper abs and obliques.

FISH OUT OF WATER

Lie down on your left side with your hands to your side and keep your feet together. Simultaneously lift your legs and your upper body while keeping your hip on the ground. Return to starting position and then perform on right side. This short contraction works on your oblique muscles.

OIL PUMPERS

Stand with your knees slightly bent and your legs shoulder-width apart. Place your right hand on the side of your head while holding a dumbbell in your left hand by your side. Lean your upper torso towards your left side as far as you can with the weight reaching towards your foot. Return to starting position then perform on right side. This movement will lengthen then contract your oblique muscles.

SWIMMERS

Lie face down on the floor. Place your arms straight above your head. Raise your right arm and left leg simultaneously as high as you can, keeping them straight as possible. Return to the starting position and repeat with your left arm and leg. A strong core reinforces good posture which means you will have better lifting technique, leading to bigger gains in strength. Swimmers work your abs, hips, and lower back without sunburn, goggles, or unflattering bathing suits....

SKYDIVERS

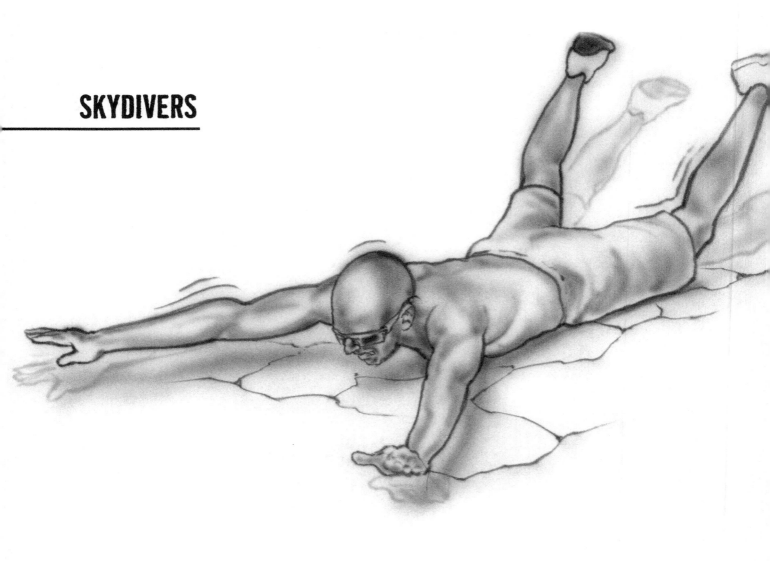

Lie face down on the floor. Place your arms straight above your head. Raise your arms and legs simultaneously as high as you can. Return to the starting position. Sky Divers train your lower back, glutes, and abs. This will give you a more stable spine and make you stronger in almost every exercise.

If you sit in front of a computer for many hours like I did to write this book you know that your muscles and connective tissues are trained to adapt to that position, giving you a hunch in your posture. You can counter that slump with Sky divers without even jumping out of a perfectly good airplane...

Get down on all fours. Extend your right leg straight out and return to the starting position. Repeat on the opposite leg. Keep your body straight and don't hyperextend your back. You don't have to be an ass to do this exercise, you just have to kick like one… Donkeys strengthen your glutes, hip-flexors, and hamstrings.

DIRTY DOGS

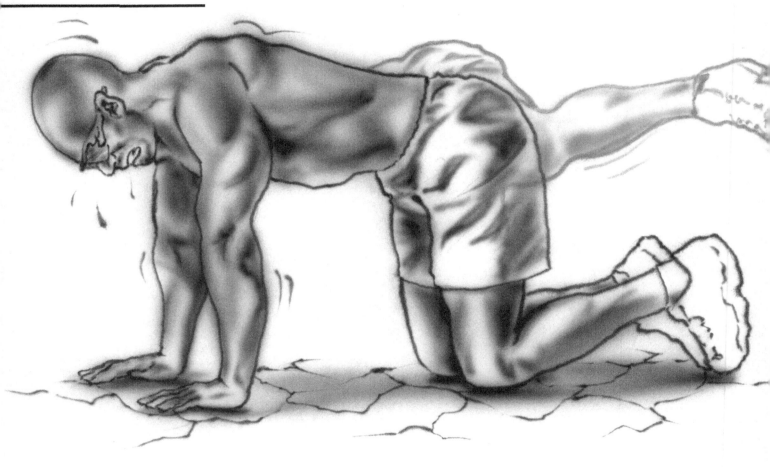

Get down on all fours. Extend your right leg out to the side, keeping your knee bent and return to the starting position. Repeat on the opposite leg. Dirty dogs work your glutes, hip flexors and core. Your glutes are the most powerful collection of muscles in your body. Since the body is one big system of muscles, when you sit on your ass all day you can negatively impact your entire muscular system by literally being a 'weak ass'… Don't pee on any fire hydrants…

STRAIGHT LEG KICKS

Get down on all fours. Extend your right leg straight out and kick out to the side, keeping your leg straight. Return to the starting position. Keep your right knee off of the ground for all of the repetitions. Repeat on the opposite leg. Straight leg kicks work your glutes, core and hip flexors.

HURDLE-HEEL CROSSOVERS

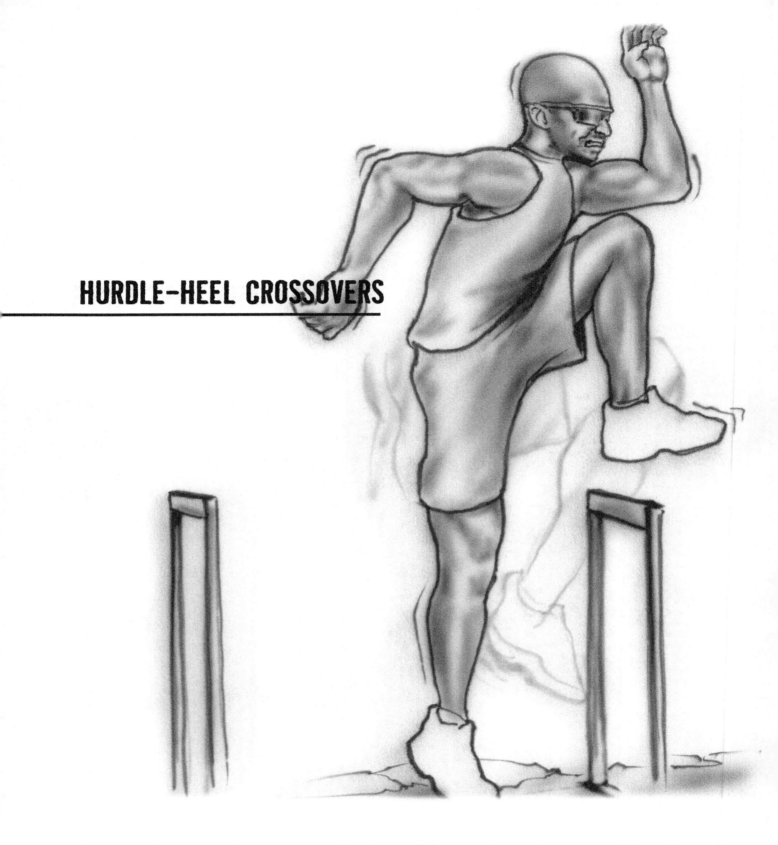

Place a hurdle at a height even with your hip. Facing the side of the hurdle raise your left heel back and forth over the edge of the hurdle. Back and over is 1 repetition. Try not to put your leg down until you finish the entire set. Repeat with the right leg. Get rid of that junk in your trunk with this hip flexor, glute-strengthening exercise that works on balance also.

HURDLE-HIP MOBILITY

Place 3 alternating high and low hurdles in straight line. Beginning at the right of the low hurdle, raise your left leg over and then your right leg. Step forward and squat underneath next high hurdle sliding to your right without bending at waist. Step forward and raise your right leg and step over the 3rd hurdle and then your left leg. This exercise strengthens your glutes and loosens your hip flexors. This helps align your pelvis and takes the stress off of your lower back. Hurdle-Hip Mobility exercises can also make you a world class limbo dancer…

HURDLE STRAIGHT-LEG SIDE SKIPS

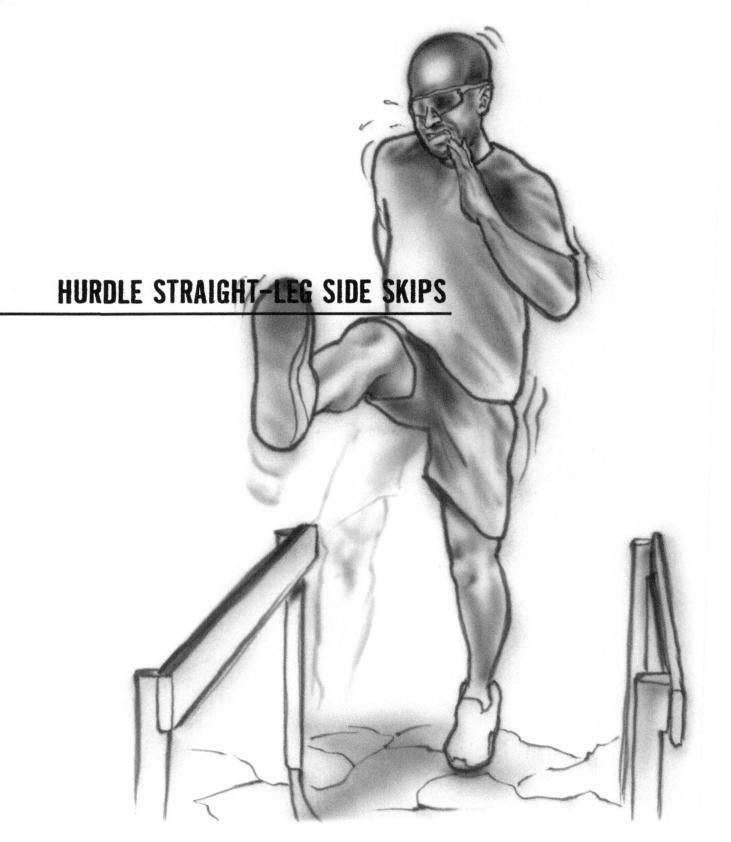

Place 6 hurdles in a straight line set at a height even with your hip. Facing the side of the 1st hurdle, perform a skip raising your left leg over the edge of each hurdle keeping your left knee bent. Repeat with the right leg. This exercise is an aerobic way to loosen up those hip flexors. If you don't have a gut and your belt still tilts toward your shoes it is because your hip flexors or too tight and your posture is being affected. These side skips work your hip flexors and stretch out your hamstrings.

HURDLE WALK-OVERS

Place 6 hurdles in a straight line set at a height even with your hip. Staying on the balls of your feet, walk over each hurdle without turning your body sideways. Hurdle walk-overs are a great way to open up your hips without having to race against Edwin Moses...

SQUATTING MUMMIES

Stand on your left leg on an 18 inch box or bench holding a light weight on your side. Bend your left knee and slowly lower your body until your right heel taps the floor. Push yourself back up using your left leg. Repeat with your right leg. Doing conventional squats with heavy weight can force you to round your back, especially when you're using a barbell. Squatting Mummies makes it easier for you to remain upright throughout the exercise. Also, as a single-leg exercise, it pushes your leg muscles harder without your having to add more weight, strengthening your entire lower body, shoulders and improves your balance. Good thing you don't have to be dead and entombed to do it…

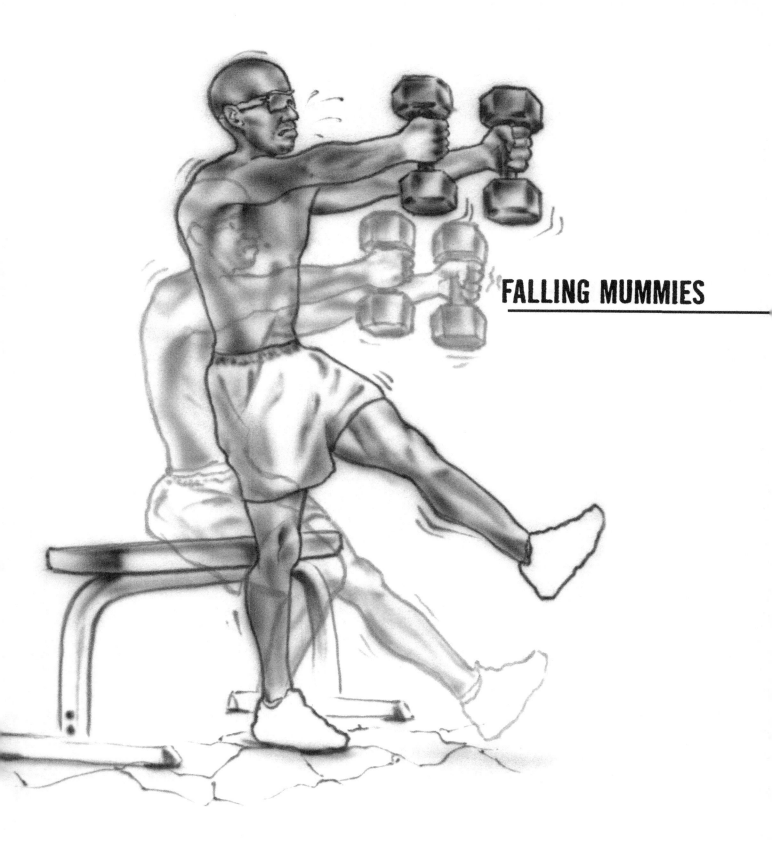

FALLING MUMMIES

Stand on your left leg on in front of an 18 inch box or bench holding a light weight on your side. Bend your left knee and slowly lower your body until your butt taps the box or bench. Push yourself back up using your left leg. Repeat with your right leg. This variation of our toilet-paper wrapped friend focuses on the same muscles as Squatting Mummies. You'll also add core strength and a shoulder raise.

STATIC LUNGES

Stand with one foot 2 to 3 feet in front of the other. Lower your body down until your knee is nearly touching the floor. Push yourself back up to the starting position. Repeat on the other leg. Drop your back knee straight down as close to the floor as possible. Also drop your torso down without leaning forward, causing your front heel to rise as you do this exercise. This will keep your weight balanced evenly through your front foot, allowing you to work the correct muscles.

JUMP LUNGES

Stand with one foot 2 to 3 feet in front of the other. Lower your body until your knee is nearly touching the floor. Jump straight up, as explosively as possible and scissor-kick your legs, landing with the opposite leg in front. Jump Lunges strengthen your shoulders and develops explosive power in your upper-body.

BACKWARD-LUNGE KNEE DRIVES

Hold a medicine ball at your chest with your elbows tucked to your side. Lunge backwards with your left foot until your left knee nearly touches the floor. As you lunge backwards, twist your upper torso to the right. As you return to the starting position, twist your torso to the left while raising your left knee. Repeat on the right side.

Putting these two exercises allows you to simultaneously train your shoulders, hips, thighs, and core. That's because switching the weight to one side of your body forces your core muscles to keep you from falling over. These lunges also burn a lot of calories and burn belly-fat.

OVERHEAD LUNGE MATRIX

Hold a medicine ball or weight over your head. Lunge forward with your left leg and return to the starting position. Perform a side lunge to the left side and return to the starting position. Repeat on the right side. This double exercise helps you improve flexibility by working lower back muscles and hip flexors. You also get the benefit of a strength-building leg routine and shoulder stability.

DROP-CATCH SQUATS

Hold a medicine ball at your chest with your elbows tucked to your side. While performing a squat, let go of the ball and catch it at the bottom of the squat. Return to the starting position. This exercise can also be used as a total-body warm-up. It will loosen your back muscles and keep your core muscles tight. You'll also increase blood flow to your arms and legs, to prepare them for a great workout.

DROP-UNDER SQUAT

Hold a medicine ball or weight at chest level with your elbows tucked to your side. While performing a squat, simultaneously press the weight overhead. Return to the starting position.

LUNGE STRIKE

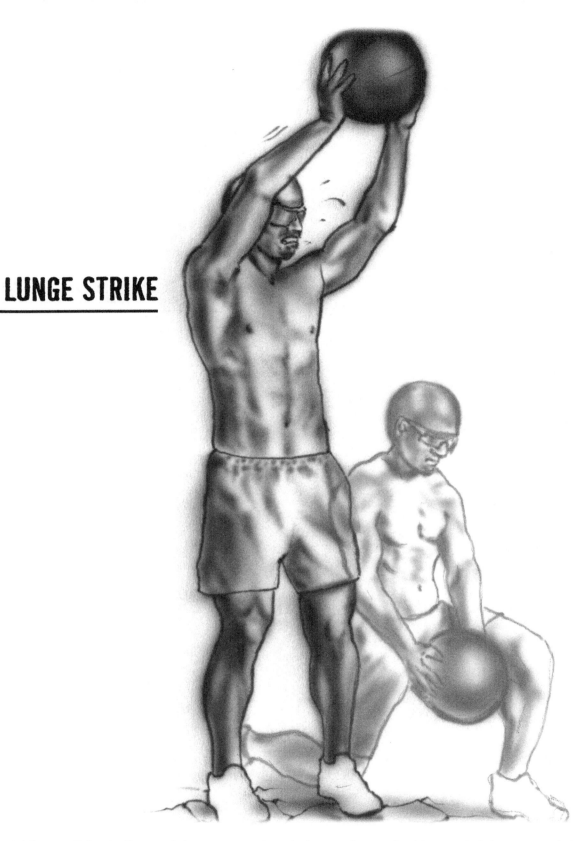

Hold a medicine ball or weight over your head. Lunge forward with your left leg as you bring the weight across your body to your left ankle. Return to the starting position. Repeat on your right side.

REBOUND-JUMP SQUATS

Hold a medicine ball or weight at your chest with your elbows tucked to your side. Perform a squat. Press the weight overhead as you jump straight up. Return to the starting position. Jump squats will improve your fitness, vertical leap and sprint times, burn more fat, and speed up your metabolism. Jump squats are an everyday exercise for frogs. In order for us to build powerful legs like amphibians, we have to loosen our lower-body joints with this exercise.

MEDICINE BALL BUCKET THROW

Hold a medicine ball with both hands at chest level with your arms extended. Squat while swinging the ball back between your legs. Explode into a standing position, throwing the ball back over your head. Turn, run and stop the ball from rolling. Repeat the exercise, throwing the ball toward the starting point. This type of throw combines a squat with an explosive shoulder movement.

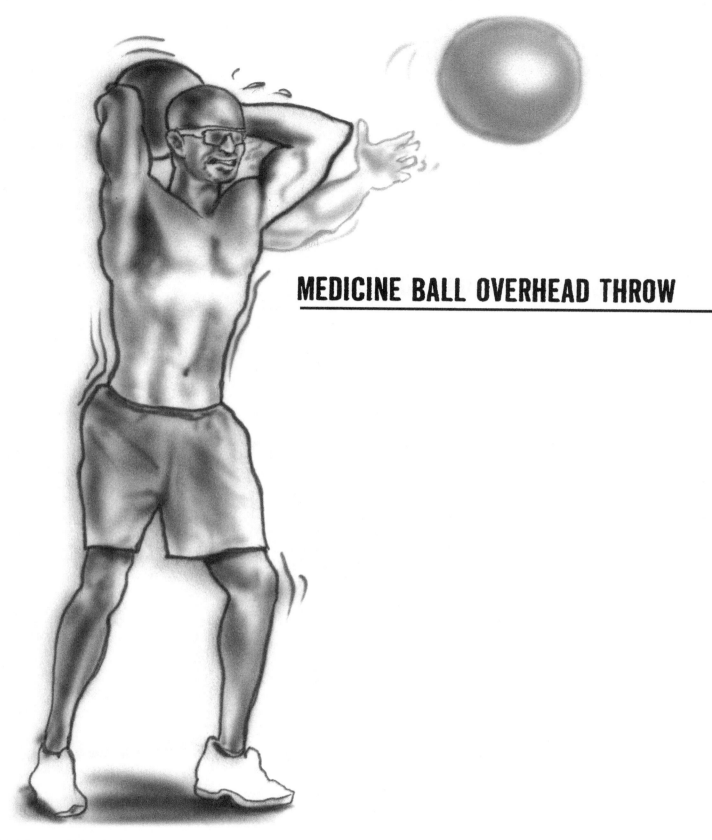

MEDICINE BALL OVERHEAD THROW

Hold a medicine ball with both hands behind your head. While lunging forward throw the ball over your head. Run and stop the ball from rolling. Repeat the exercise, throwing the ball toward the starting point. This cardio-explosive routine is designed to help you build a rock-solid core, burn fat, and improve your sports performance.

MOGUL TWIST-SQUAT JUMPS

Hold a pair of dumbbells at your side and stand with your feet and lower body turned 45 degrees to your left. Perform a squat, jump, and turn your lower body and upper body in opposite directions, landing with your lower body turned to the right. The explosion and change of direction in this type of squat trains your muscles from every angle, speeding growth and improving stability.

BALANCE BOARD SQUATS

Hold your arms out for balance and stand tall on a balance board with your feet shoulder-width apart. Lower your body as far as you can by pushing your hips back and bending your knees. Push back up to the starting position. Working out on balance boards help you work on maintaining your sense of balance and maintaining a low center of gravity which is ideal for sports requiring good balance like skiing, surfing, stand-up paddle boarding, and others.

DUMBBELL FRONT SQUATS

Hold a pair of dumbbells in the curl position near the top of your shoulders. Squat down, keeping your torso as upright as possible. Do not allow your elbows to drop. Front squats are a more advanced move than back squats. Sit back between your legs instead of on top of your knees. Start the lift by pushing your hips back instead of bending your knees first, which puts more stress on the joints.

When you squat, imagine you're standing on a piece of paper. Try to rip the paper apart by pressing your feet hard into the floor and outward. This activates your glutes, which helps you to go heavier and take stress off of the joints around the knees.

The weight rests on the fronts of your shoulders, helping to keep your back upright.
Research has shown that those who squat long-term have tighter, stronger knee ligaments than those who skip this all-around muscle builder. Squats place less stress on your knees than a leg extension machine. The closer you come to a half squat (lowering your body until your thighs are parallel to the floor) the harder you work your quads, hamstrings, and calf muscles. To squat safely, keep your back as upright as possible and lower your body until your thighs are parallel to the floor or as far as you can go without feeling it in your knees.

I love squats because it is one of the most effective exercises you can do. It works almost every muscle in your body, including your core, and burns serious calories. Your hips and knees bend at the same time to complete the lift. Squats release more of the key hormones that increase strength and muscle and decrease body fat. The heavier the squats, the best way to build pure, functional strength, because they not only exercise your muscles, but also force the network of nerves controlling them to work better. Great form is the key.

When doing back squats, rest the bar so that as much of it as possible is touching our shoulders. If you hold it only on your lower neck area it can cause the entire weight to compress your spine, which can lead to muscle and spinal injuries.

Keep your heels on the floor when you squat. If you can't, work on exercises to loosen up your hip flexors.

STRAIGHT-LEG DEADLIFT

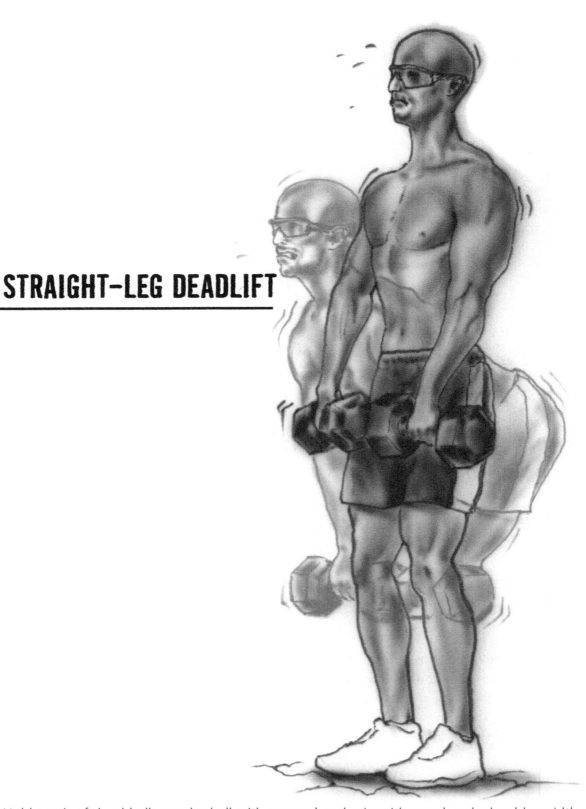

Hold a pair of dumbbells or a barbell with an overhand grip with your hands shoulder-width apart. Without moving your legs, bend at your hips and lower the weight as low as you can and return to the starting position. Push your hips back and keep your lower back straight. If you round your lower back as you bend over you will put yourself at risk for back problems. When you lower the bar, keep it close to your legs like you are shaving using the bar. The farther the bar is away from your body the more it places strain on your back, which increases your chance of injury and limits the emphasis on your hamstrings and glutes. As you lift the bar, squeeze your glutes like two fists. You'll ensure that you're engaging your butt muscles. This helps you generate more power, lift more weight, and produce better results.

DEADLIFTS

Load a barbell or hold a pair of dumbbells and let them rest against your shins. Bend at your hips, keeping your back straight and grab the weight at shoulder width with an overhand grip. Pull your torso back and up and pull your hips forward to stand up with the barbell. Keep your back straight. Lower the weight back to the starting position, keeping it as close to your body as possible. The dead lift is still the top exercise for developing total-body strength and muscle. The dead lift works wonders on your body for the exact reason the exercises 'haters' avoid doing it. It requires a combined effort from hundreds of muscles, including those in your lower back.

STEP-UPS

Stand in front of a bench or 18 inch box and place your left foot on the bench or box. Press your left heel into the box or bench, pushing your body up until your left leg is straight. Step down and repeat with your right leg. Adding a step-up routine to your squats and lunges will train the hamstrings as hip extensors and strengthen your glutes as well.

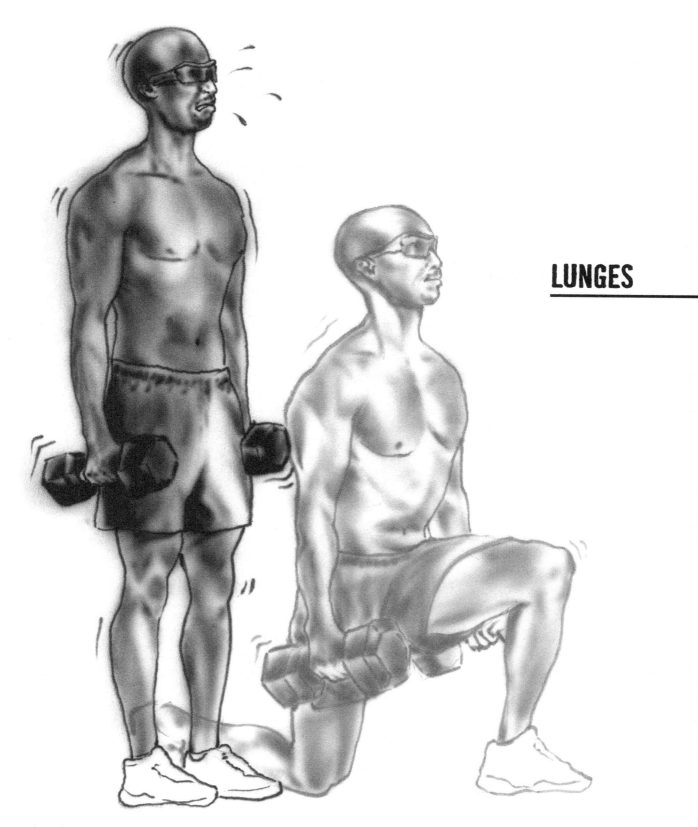

LUNGES

Step forward with your left leg and lower your body until your knee is bent at 90 degrees. Push off your left foot back to the starting position, keeping your torso straight. Repeat with your right leg. When you lunge and keep your torso upright, focus on moving it up and down, not backward and forward. This will keep your weight balanced evenly through your front foot, allowing you to press hard into the floor with your heel and target more muscle. To add a core workout with Lunges, narrow your starting stance. The smaller the gap between your feet, the more your core has to work to keep your body stabilized.

CALF RAISES

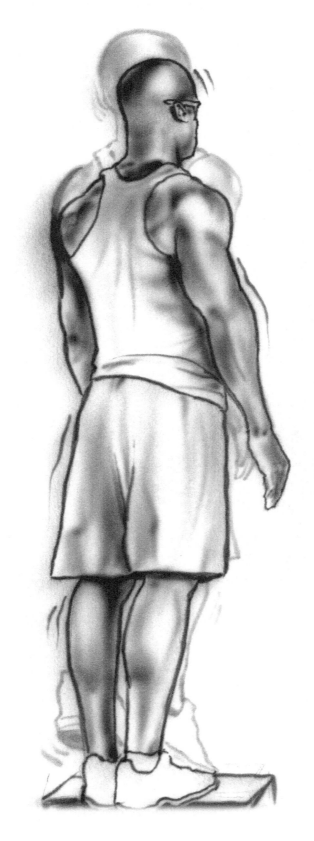

Grab a pair of dumbbells or place a barbell across your upper back. Stand on a 25lb. plate on the balls of your feet. Rise up on your toes as high as you can. Return to the starting position. Do seated and standing calf raises. You will get better results. Calves are made up of two different muscles so you must do the seated and straight-leg versions of the exercise to hit them both.

DECLINE-SPIDERMAN PUSH-UPS

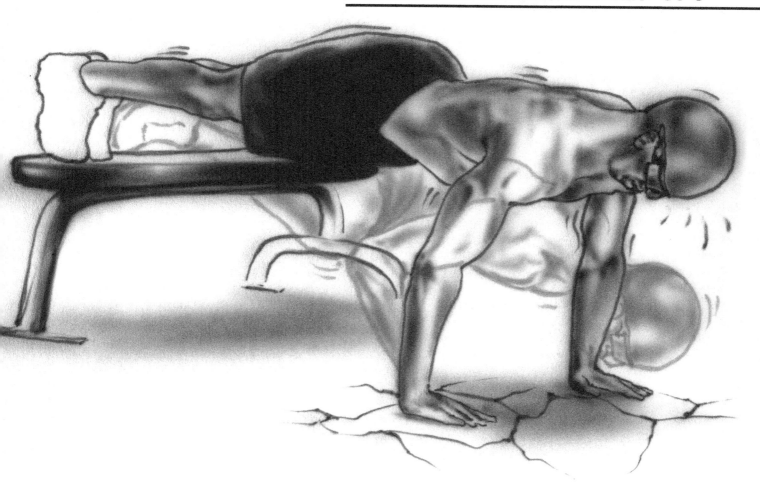

Get in the push-up position with your feet on a bench. While lowering yourself down, keep your elbow close to your side and pull your left knee towards your elbow. Push yourself back up to the starting position. Repeat on the right side.

You might not be able to shoot spider webs to buildings and swing around, but you will strengthen your upper body and increases mobility in your hips and shoulders which will help you squeeze into your super-hero suit…

"T" PUSH-UPS

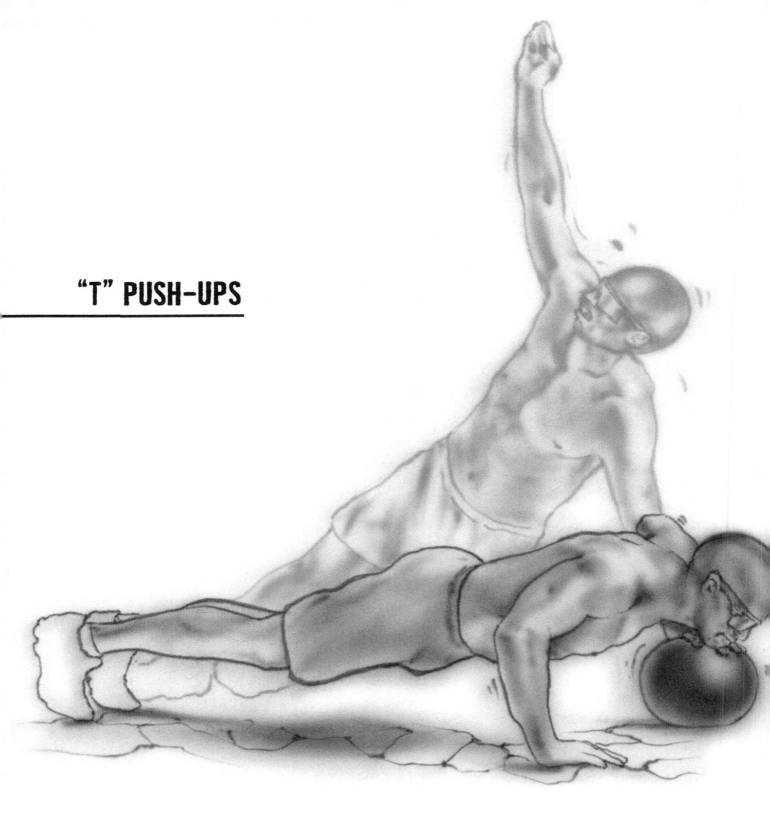

Hold a pair of dumbbells in the push-up position. Lower yourself to the floor keeping your elbows close to your side. As you push back up, rotate the left side of your body sideways, pulling your left arm straight above you forming a "t". Return to the start and repeat on the right side. This core move will not only work your chest and shoulders, but just about every other muscle in your body.

BALANCE BOARD PUSH-UPS

Get down in the push-up position with your hands just outside of your shoulders on a balance board. Lower your body until your chest touches the board keeping your elbows close to your side. Push yourself back up to the starting position. Keep your body in a straight line from head to ankles. The instability of a balance board will make all the muscle stabilizers in your shoulder and chest work overtime.

SPORTS BALL PUSH-UPS

Get in the push-up position with both of your hands on a sports ball, Swiss ball or medicine ball. Lower your body until your chest touches the ball while keeping your elbows close to your side and push yourself back up to the starting position. Keep your body in a straight line from head to ankles. When you place your hands on a medicine ball or Swiss ball and balance yourself, the instability causes your core muscles to work much harder than when you do push-ups on the floor. You will train the muscles of your midsection and hips to remain stable longer. As a result, you will be able to do more push-ups and work more muscle.

PUSH-UP ROWS

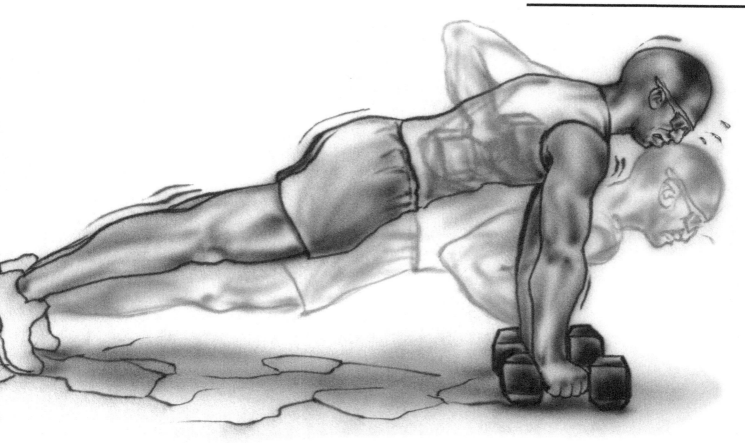

Get in the push-up position while holding dumbbells. Perform a push-up keeping your elbows close to your side. As you push back up to starting position, pull a dumbbell to the outside of your chest and lower it down. Repeat this move with the other arm. The push-up row is one of the best overall upper body exercises you can do. In two moves you work your back, biceps, chest, triceps, shoulders and core.

PERFECT PUSH-UPS

Get in the push-up position with both of your hands shoulder-width apart, gripping a pair of perfect push-ups in the horizontal position. Lower your body, keeping your elbows close to your side while twisting the perfect push-ups to a vertical position until your chest nears the floor and push yourself back up to the starting position. Keep your body in a straight line from head to ankles. When you're in a pushup position, your posture should look the same as it would if you were standing up straight and tall. Do not let your hips sag and round out your upper back.

Before you start, suck in your stomach like you are trying to get into some tight pants and hold it that way for the entire range of motion. This will help your body remain tight with perfect posture as you perform the exercise. Most guys seem to abandon the push-up for the bench press sometime around the time they start noticing girls…

DUMBBELL FLY

Lie on your back on a Swiss Ball or a bench holding a pair of dumbbells over your chest with a slight bend in your elbows. Lower the dumbbells out and away from your chest until they are parallel with your chest while squeezing your back muscles together. Pull the dumbbells back to the starting position.

INCLINE DUMBBELL PRESS

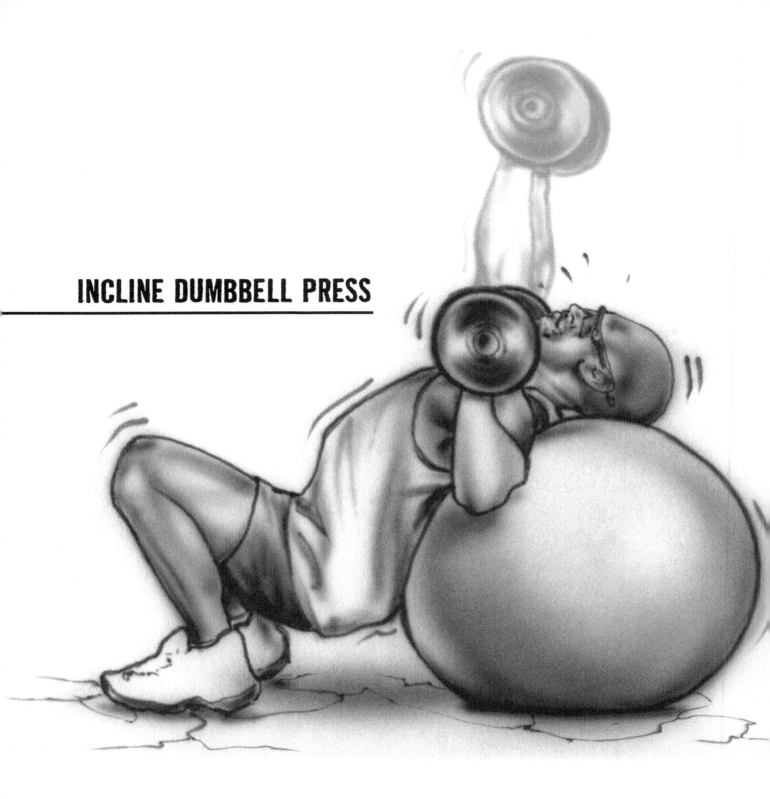

Place your back on a Swiss ball or an incline bench with your torso angled at 45 degrees. Hold the dumbbells straight up at chin level with your arms extended. Lower the dumbbells just outside your shoulders and press them back up to the starting position. Lowering the weight too far puts too much stress on the shoulder joints.

The incline dumbbell press works the upper part of your chest. It also strengthens your front shoulders, triceps, and the muscles that help move your shoulder blades.

Hold the bars on a dip station and lift your body until your arms are straight. Lower yourself by bending your elbows and keeping them close to your side until your shoulders are parallel to your elbows. Push yourself back up to the starting position. Dips are a great exercise for building your chest and triceps, but lean forward to avoid shoulder pain.

DOUBLE-PLATE PRESS

Press 2 plates together with the smooth sides facing outside. Spread your fingers wide but not over the edges of the plates. Hold the plates at chest level and extend your arms outward, keeping your elbows close to your side and then return them to chest level. This unique exercise strengthens your chest, biceps, shoulders, abs, and grip. Just remember to keep those feet shoulder width apart or it can have the same result as Toe Busters…

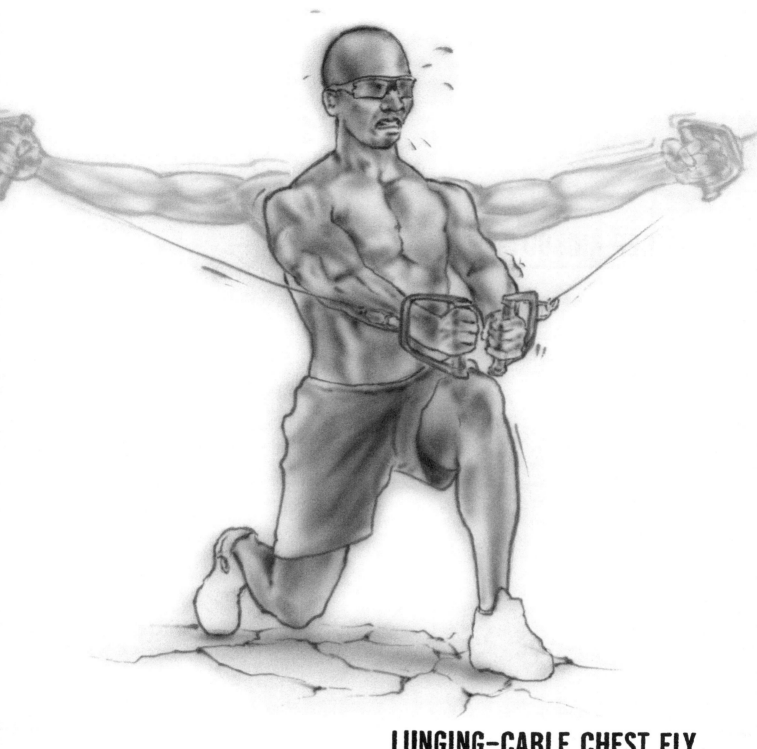

LUNGING-CABLE CHEST FLY

Attach two stirrup handles to the high-pulley cables. Grab a handle with each hand. While performing a lunge, pull the handles down and together until they cross in front of your chest without changing the angle of your elbows. This is a total body exercise that works: biceps, chest, shoulders, legs, back and core in two moves!

TRICEP KICKOUTS

Place your left hand and left knee on a bench. Holding a dumbbell in your right hand, your upper right arm and torso should be parallel to the floor with your elbow bent. Raise your right forearm until your arm is completely straight, without moving your upper arm. Lower it back down to the starting position and repeat with the left arm. This is a great way to work the triceps, which accounts for 60% of the upper arm although most people work their biceps more.

SKULL CRUSHERS

Start by keeping your body parallel at a 45 degree angle. Keep your arms extended, gripping a bar with an overhand grip. Slowly lower yourself until your forehead is close to the bar keeping your elbows in tight to your side. Push yourself back up to the starting position. Might want to wear a helmet…

TRICEP PRESS-DOWN

Hold the end of a rope with each hand, keeping your hands shoulder-width apart and your elbows close to your side. Pull the rope down rotating your wrists without moving your upper arms or leaning forward until your elbows are locked. Return to the starting position. Don't use too much weight or you will depend on your shoulder and back muscles to do all of the work.

BICEP, HAMMER AND REVERSE CURLS

Hold a pair of dumbbells or a curl bar with an underhand grip for bicep curls, an overhand grip for reverse curls, or with your palms facing each other for hammer curls. Let the weight hang at arm's length straight down from your shoulders. Without moving your upper arms, bend your elbows and curl the weight as close to your shoulders as possible. Lower the weights back to the starting position. Bend your wrists to work your biceps harder. Extend your wrists backward and hold them that way when you do arm curls. When doing standing arm curls, completely straighten your arms by flexing your triceps at the end of each repetition. This makes sure that you work the muscle through its entire range of motion.

The underhand grip will work the largest muscle on the front part of your arm. The reverse grip really targets your forearm. The hammer grip will give your arms thickness.

TOE BUSTERS

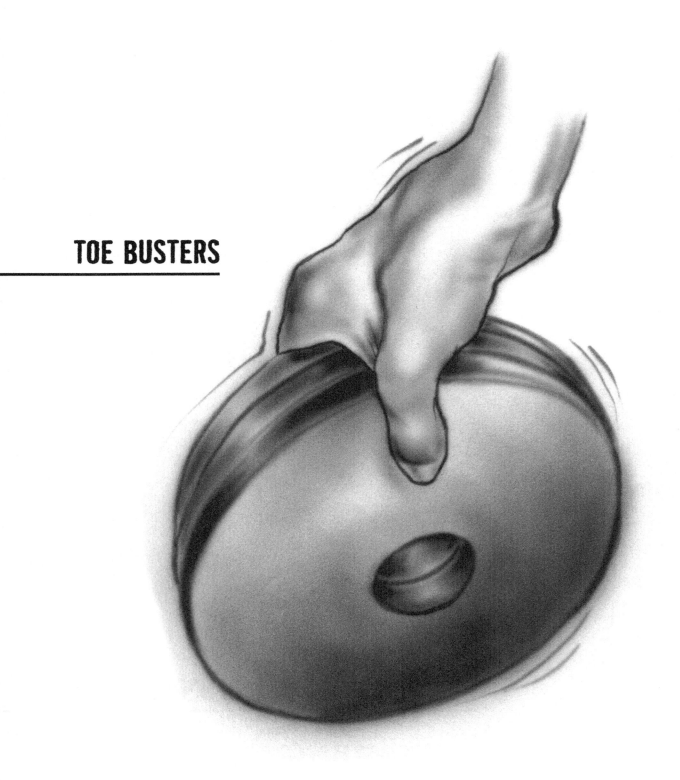

Using the tips of your fingers, squeeze and hold 2 plates together with the smooth sides facing outside. A strong grip can translate to huge gains. Don't let a weak grip cause you to lower the amount of weight you are working with because you can't hold it in your hand. The hand has 34 muscles in it. Toe Busters will work a lot of them, but please hold the weight over a bench or you will find out how it got its name...

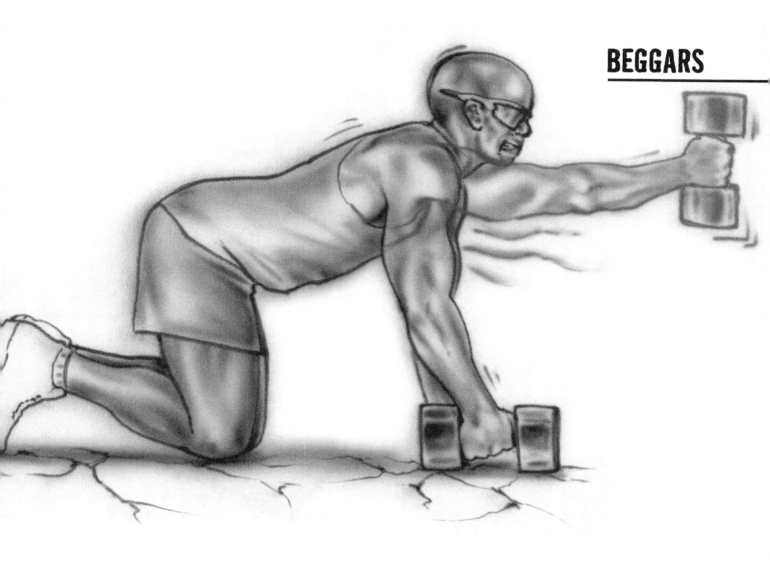

BEGGARS

Get on your hands and knees, holding a light weight in your right hand. Lean forward, shifting your weight on your left hand. Keeping your right arm straight, lift the weight to shoulder level and return it to the floor. Repeat on the left side. This sneaky exercise surprises you by giving you a great core workout, as well as your back and shoulders. Too bad the dumbbell won't hold spare change…

REVERSE-GRIP SHOULDER PRESS

Sit on a balance ball or bench holding a pair of dumbbells at shoulder height, with your arms bent and palms facing your shoulders. Press the dumbbells upward, rotating your palms 90 degrees until they are facing out. The function of this exercise is to work all the muscles that hold your upper-arm bone in its socket and allow the shoulder blade to move.

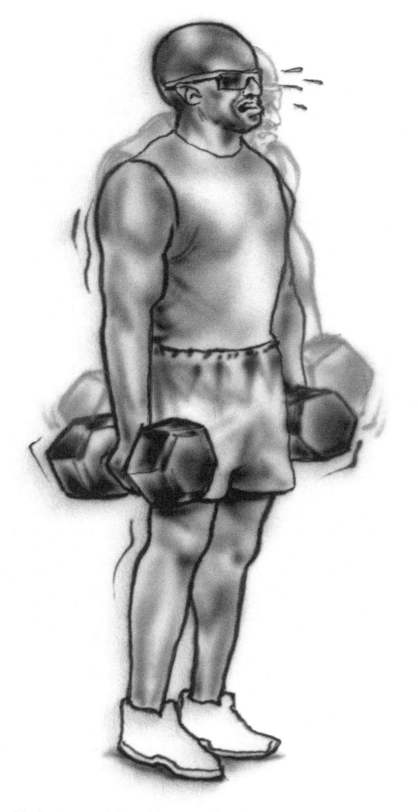

SHRUGS

Hold a pair of dumbbells at your sides with your palms facing each other and let them hang by your side. Shrug your shoulders and return to the starting position. Shrugs target your upper traps, which are responsible for rotating your shoulder blades upward and the muscles that run down the back of your neck which rotate your shoulder blades downward. These muscles give you great posture.

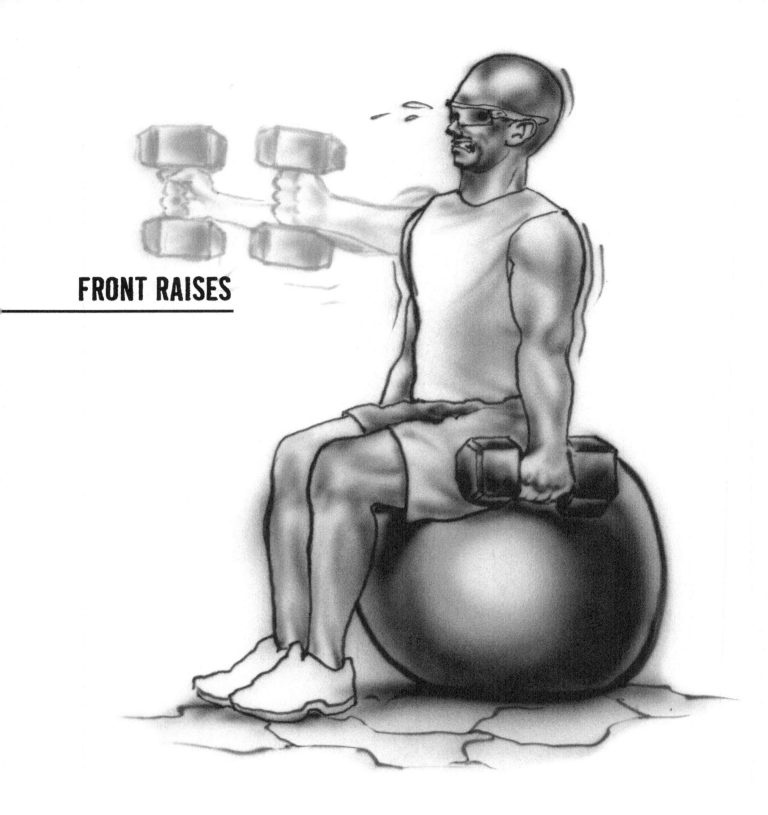

FRONT RAISES

Perform this raise, standing up, holding dumbbells at your sides. Lift the dumbbells straight out in front of you to shoulder level, keeping your arms straight. Lower the weight to the starting position. Bouldering up your shoulders is one of the keys to making your waist look slimmer, your arms bigger, and your back V-shaped.

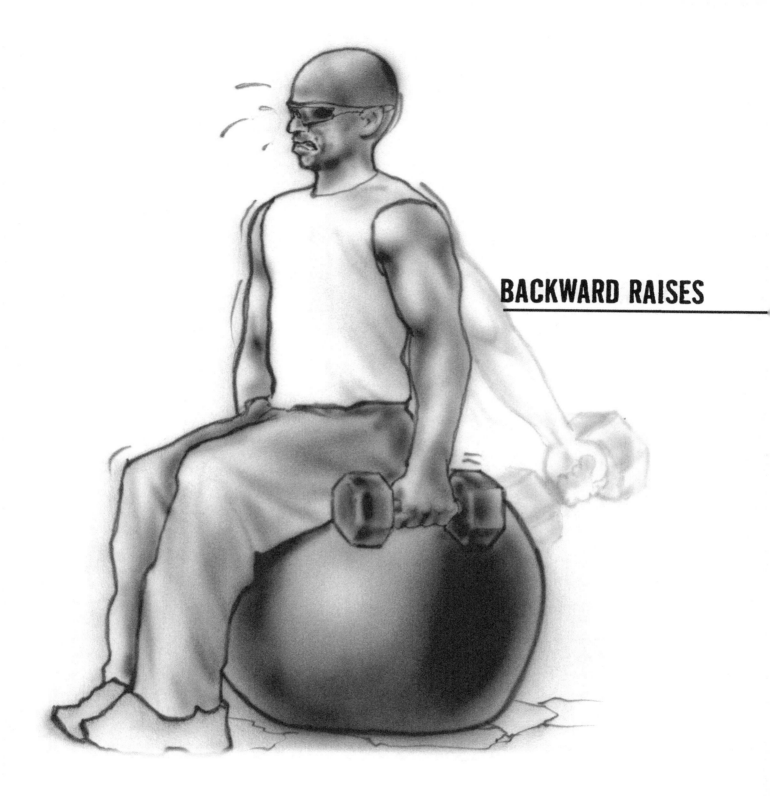

BACKWARD RAISES

Start this raise by holding dumbbells at your sides. Lift the dumbbells straight behind you as high as you can, keeping your arms straight without leaning forward. Lower the weight to the starting position. By attacking the weakest part of the shoulder muscles tat surround your shoulder joint, these raises reduce your risk of a dislocation or tear in your rotator cuff.

LATERAL RAISES

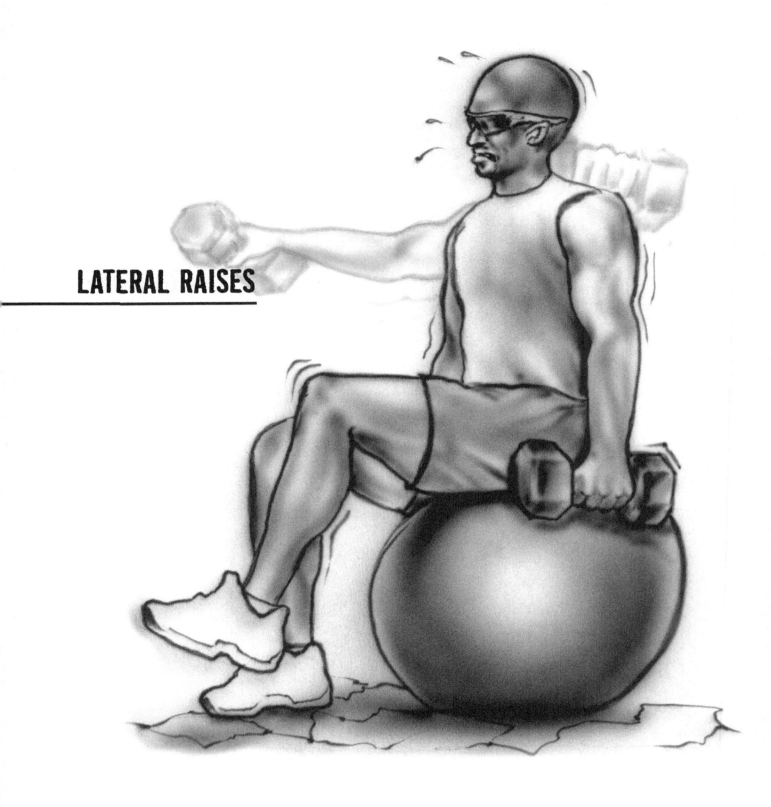

Perform this raise by holding dumbbells at your sides with your palms facing outward. Lift the dumbbells straight out to your sides until they are shoulder level. Lower the weight to the starting position. Lateral raise targets the rear part of your shoulder which is also the weakest. Many injuries can occur because your muscles are out of balance. These raises improve your stabilizing muscles and protect your rotator cuff.

STEERING WHEELS

Hold a plate straight out in front of you, chest level, keeping your arms straight. Turn the plate 180 degrees clock-wise then counter clock-wise for each repetition. The rotation in this routine conditions your cardiovascular system and builds bigger muscle in the last place your body looks to store fat: your shoulders. Steering wheels are also a good way to strengthen the muscles around your rotator cuff. Now you can turn a big rig with no power steering…

ARM CIRCLES

Hold a pair of dumbbells out to the side at shoulder level. Make small, circular rotations forward or backward. This is a great exercise to maintain flexibility in your shoulders. This is important since the shoulder is the most unstable joint in your body.

SHOULDER PUSH-UPS

Assume a push-up position with your feet on a bench. Push your hips up so your torso is almost perpendicular to the floor. Lower your body until your head almost touches the floor. Return to the starting position. Unlike the standard push-up, the shoulder push-up places most of the workload on your shoulders and triceps, while reducing the demand on your chest.

LAT PULL-DOWNS

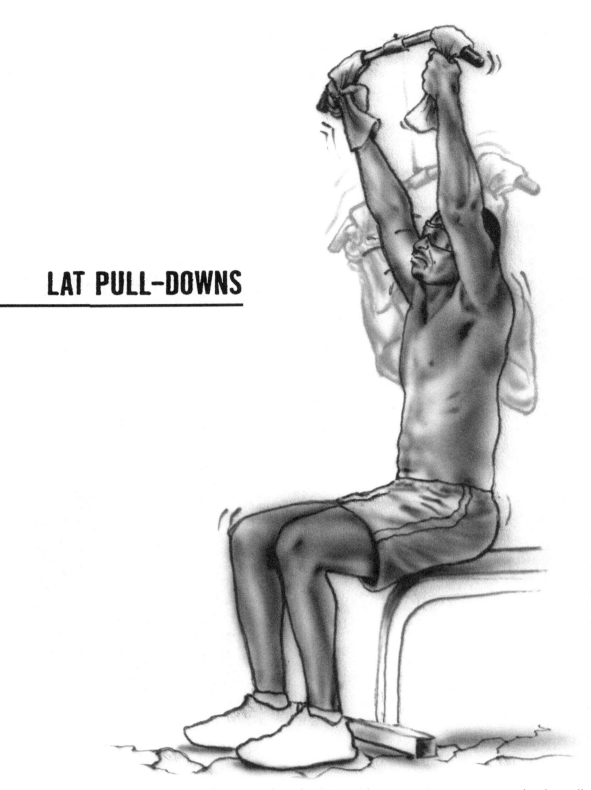

Grab the bar or towels with an overhand grip. Without moving your upper body, pull the bar down to your chest, squeezing your shoulder blades together. Try to imagine that there's a quarter between your shoulder blades and you need to squeeze it in order to keep it from falling as you pull the weight down. Return to the starting position. When doing lat pull-downs, don't wrap your thumb around the bar. Instead, place it next to your other fingers. This will decrease the involvement of your arm muscles, so your back will work harder. Try this for pull-ups also.

Pull- downs are great for more than just your back. They also help build your shoulders, abs and even your biceps. If you can't complete a pull-up, you won't build your back muscles to their full potential. So do lat pull downs to develop strength in this range of motion.

REVERSE DUMBBELL FLY

Lie face down on a Swiss ball or bench. Raise the dumbbells straight out to the side until they are parallel to your body. Return to the starting position.

REVERSE PUSH-UPS

Position a Barbell 3 feet off of the Ground. Get underneath the bar and grab it bar with an over-hand grip with your hands shoulder-width apart. Hang with your arms and body straight with your feet resting on top of a Swiss ball or bench. Pull your shoulder blades back and pull until your chest reaches the bar, creating as much space between your chin and shoulders as you can. This will make sure you're working the middle and upper-back muscles.

LAWN MOWER STARTERS

Holding a dumbbell in your right hand with your arm straight, place your left hand and left knee on a bench. Use your upper-back muscles to pull the dumbbell up and back toward your hip. Pull the weight high enough where your elbow passes your torso. As you pull the weight, stick your chest out, this will allow you to better retract your shoulder blades which will lead to better results. Return to the starting position. Now go cut the grass…

DUMBBELL PULL-OVERS

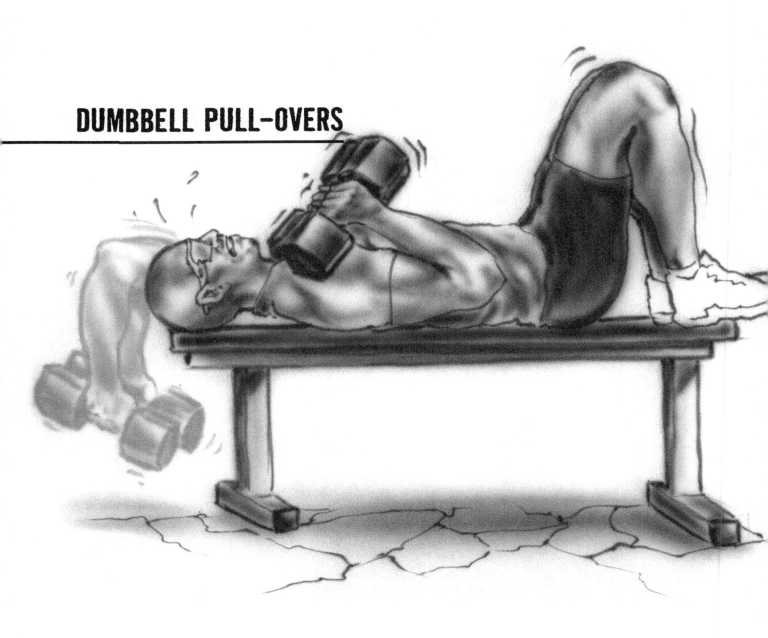

Lying with your upper back on a Swiss ball or bench, hold a dumbbell with two hands over your face. Lower the dumbbell behind your head, keeping your elbows in tight. Return to the starting position.

1-ARM CABLE PULL-DOWNS

While on your knees, grab a cable with an over-hand grip with your right arm extended. Pull the cable down to your shoulder, twisting your arm to a curl position. Repeat with your left arm.

SPIDERMANS

Crawl down steps or benches, leading with your hands. This is my signature exercise. A total body exercise that really works your core, hip flexors, shoulders, legs and chest. While crawling down, reach with your hand first allowing your momentum to pull your feet behind you. Only one foot and hand is allowed to touch each step at one time. Now we can protect Gotham City…

BOX HOPS

With a dumbbell in each hand, jump on top of an 18 inch box while simultaneously lifting the dumbbells to your shoulders. Step down and repeat.

UMBRELLAS

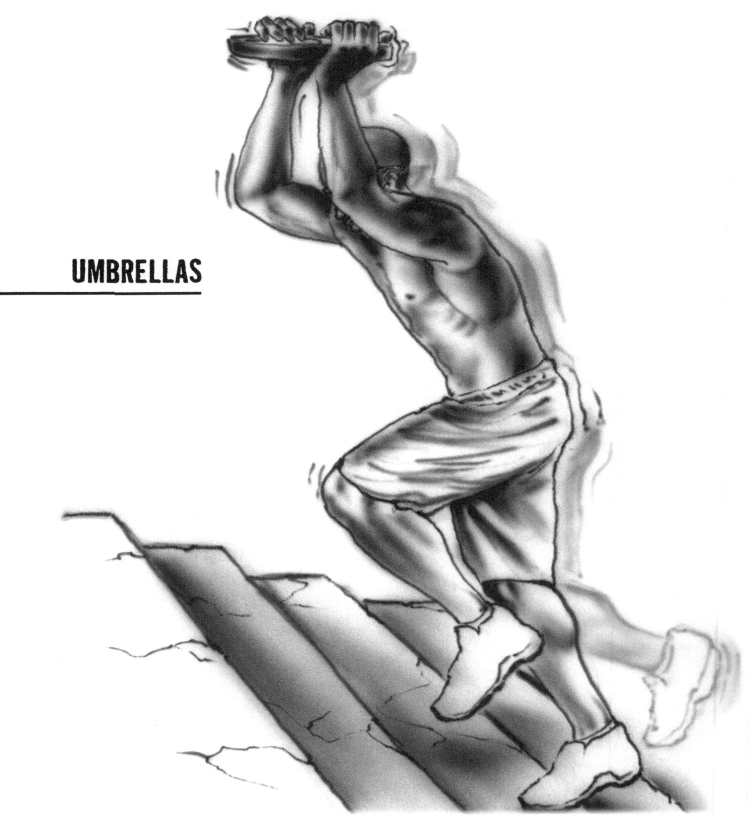

Holding a plate or medicine ball over your head, lunge up every other step. The weight can actually shield you from getting wet if you choose to do these in the rain…

PARACHUTE SPRINTS

Begin by jogging from a standstill. Slowly pick up speed to allow the shoot to open gradually, providing light resistance until you get to a full sprint, creating strong resistance.

SLED SPRINTS

Begin by jogging from a standstill. Slowly pick up speed, providing light resistance until you get to a full sprint, creating strong resistance. Pushing a sled and doing other drills like it will increase your strength on some of the exercises that you normally do. Your squat will go up and your chest strength will improve. The sled builds your hamstrings and butt muscles, which are the key muscles for speed.

BUNGEE SPRINTS

Begin by jogging from a standstill. Slowly pick up speed to allow the bungee to stretch out gradually, providing light resistance until you get to a full sprint, creating strong resistance.

MOUNTAIN CLIMBERS

Get in the push-up position with your arms straight. Lift your right foot and raise your knee as close to your chest as you can. Tap the ground with your right foot and then return to the starting position and repeat with your left leg. Go as fast as possible. You won't be going up Mt. Everest, but you will be strong enough to. Leave your hiking boots, gloves and pick axe at home…

WINDSHIELD WIPER SLIDES

Get in the pushup position with your toes on the slide board. Spread your legs as wide apart as possible and back together again as quickly as possible.

LONG SLIDES

Stand at one edge of the Slide Board. From this position push out as if you are skating. Practice good form and control. Vary the angle of your pushing leg to increase range of motion.

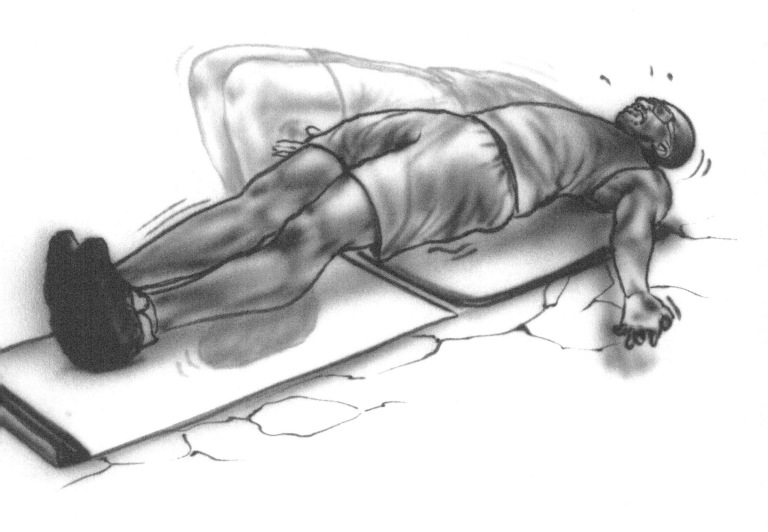

LEG CURL SLIDES

Lie on the slide face up with your feet flat and your heels underneath your butt. Keeping your upper torso and butt in the air the entire time, slide your heels out until your legs are straight. Reverse this movement back to the starting position. Leg curl slides are a great way to train your calves, hamstrings and core muscles in your lower back.

KERMIT CANNON

Kermit Cannon, the strength and conditioning coach of Santa Monica High School, has been running "Beast Factory" boot camps for students and athletes twice a day since 1993.

He is the owner of Youth Sports Training, a company that gives young athletes the skills and training that will help them perform at a higher, healthier level. Cannon's mission is to teach youth to train properly and play smart. He also strives to educate parents to begin or successfully continue guiding their children on the road of health, fitness, and sports.

His workouts emphasize how fitness can be achieved through an approach that enhances the mind, strengthens the body, and nurtures the spirit; he encourages achieving the proper balance in pursuit of a totally fit lifestyle.

He has trained hundreds of individuals and several teams in many different sports, several of them going on to receive college athletic scholarships and many have gone on to have professional sports careers.

Kermit is a member of Men's Health FitSchools and the White House's Let's Move! non-profit organizations. Kermit is a 2011 recipient of the President's Council on Fitness, Sports & Nutrition Community Leadership Award.

BRIAN GARCIA, A.K.A. "TAZROC"

Brian Garcia, a.k.a."Tazroc", was born in Eugene, Oregon. At the age of 14, he developed a passion for drawing after being inspired by his uncle's prison artwork and by graffiti he saw in many major cities of the U.S. while performing and competing in bicycle freestyle competitions.

His artwork is heavily influenced by his Chicano culture. In 1987, Brian started painting graffiti art, turning what started out as a hobby into a dream job. Wanting to expand his career as an artist, he moved to Los Angeles in 2000 and started his own business painting custom murals on low riders. Many of his clients were in the entertainment industry, and this eventually led him to movie sets, music videos, and commercials.

Brian is an acclaimed graffiti artist, known by many for his spray can photorealism. His urban art has been featured in numerous commercials, music videos, ad campaigns, and at charity events.

He is one of the most sought after spray can artists on the West Coast, with a notable list of clients that include Snoop Dogg, Pepsi, Boost Mobile, Max Payne, Rihanna, Jay Z, Beyonce, Usher, Brittney Spears, Justin Timberlake, Muscle Milk, Subway, Honda, Verizon, Footaction, Gatorade, Reebok, Ecko Unlimited., and Sony Inc. and Hyundai.

Brian's talent has been commissioned by art galleries in and around Los Angeles. Brian educates inner city youth through art events and workshops in an effort to allow them artistic expression and provide them with a creative outlet. He has been a significant force in gaining respect for graffiti as a valid art form.

Made in the USA
Monee, IL
12 January 2021